CAMBRIDGE
UNIVERSITY PRESS

Cambridge Global English

LEARNER'S BOOK 9

Chris Barker & Libby Mitchell

Contents

Use of English	Cross-curricular links	Vocabulary	21st-century skills
-ing forms Present simple and present continuous Present simple passive Present continuous passive	Psychology Media studies	Classroom interaction Character and behaviour	Social responsibilities: Be aware of positive behaviour at school and at home; encourage others to participate in and contribute to projects; understand how personal habits and behaviour have the capacity to affect others Critical thinking: Compare points and arguments from different sources; identify assumptions and inferences in an argument Creative thinking: Plan and give a presentation on teenage life; interpret a photo Collaborative working: Pair work, group work, projects
Abstract nouns Comparative adjectives and adverbs *Must have, might have, can't have* + past participle Strong adjectives and intensifiers	Science and medicine Psychology	Food and health Feelings and emotions	Social responsibilities: Make informed choices in relation to diet and health; understand the contribution of other cultures to our lives Critical thinking: Give reasons for the plausibility of conclusions about health and happiness Learning to learn: Work out the meaning of words from their context Collaborative working: Pair work, group work, projects
Compound nouns Multi-word verbs (phrasal and prepositional verbs) Past continuous passive Compound adjectives Participle adjectives	European art and architecture Environmental studies	Holidays Responsible tourism	Social responsibilities: Understand the impact tourism can have on the environment Critical thinking: Take part in a debate about the effects of tourism Creative thinking: Imagine and write a scene to continue a story Learning to learn: Take notes on what someone says Collaborative working: Pair work, group work, projects
Conjunctions Present and past simple passive Present perfect continuous Present perfect active and passive Dependent prepositions following verbs	Medical science Environmental science	Sight and colour DNA and genetics Farming and animals Zoos	Social responsibilities: Understand how disease can spread, including pandemic diseases; be aware of the importance of medical science; understand the importance of conservation Critical thinking: Distinguish between fact and opinion, and identify bias Creative thinking: Add arguments to a debate on endangered species; add ideas to a debate Learning to learn: Work out the meaning of words from their context Collaborative working: Pair work, group work, projects
Relative clauses Expressing the future *to have something done* future continuous	Technology Ancient history	Social media Ideas for presents	Social responsibilities: Understand the contribution of technology to society; understand the contribution of other cultures in history, and the role of international co-operation Creative thinking: Decide which developments in technology will be important and create a timeline for them Critical thinking: Assess the advantages and disadvantages of developments in technology; distinguish between fact and opinion Collaborative working: Pair work, group work, projects

Contents

Use of English	Cross-curricular links	Vocabulary	21st-century skills
Verbs in the passive followed by the infinitive Reported questions and statements Third conditional Past continuous	Business studies Citizenship	School rules Family rules Rights and responsibilities	Social responsibilities: Be aware of positive behaviour at school and out of school; understand rights and responsibilities Critical thinking: Evaluate ways of organising family life; compare attitudes to the law; analyse and respond to difficult situations Creative thinking: Consider how the same event or situation can be interpreted in different ways Collaborative working: Pair work, group work, projects
Past perfect simple and past perfect continuous Comparatives and superlatives Past perfect simple, active and passive Connectives	Physical education Photography	The advantages of sports Competition	Social responsibility: Be aware of the value of competitive and non-competitive sports and activities, and of international co-operation in sport and games Creative thinking: Write a description of a competition Critical thinking: Identify bias in an argument Learning to learn: Make notes in order to give a description of an event Collaborative working: Pair work, group work, projects
Adverbs of frequency Multi-word verbs Verbs followed by *-ing* Complex noun phrases	Environmental science	Weather Climate change and the environment Eco products	Social responsibilities: Understand the choices people make in relation to environmental products and sustainable living; be aware of global warming and climate change; understand how personal habits and behaviour affect the environment Critical thinking: Summarise the key points of what someone talks about; evaluate ideas for sustainable living Creative thinking: Make a short video clip about the environment and ideas for sustainability Learning to learn: Learn techniques for participating in an extended discussion Collaborative working: Pair work, group work, projects
Relative clauses Connectives Participle clauses Reported speech – statements (revision) Dependent prepositions following adjectives	Economics Medical science and psychology	Jobs Inspirational people Adjectives to describe people	Social responsibilities: Appreciate the positive aspects of celebrity; understand and value cultural and educational difference Critical thinking: Identify inconsistency and bias in what people say; recognise the difference between fact and opinion; evaluate ideas about achievement Creative thinking: Write a letter to your 21-year-old self; write dialogues to continue a story Collaborative working: Pair work, group work, projects

How to use this book

In this book you will find lots of different features to help your learning.

What you will learn in the unit or lesson.

> **In this lesson you will...**
> - **listen to** views on talking in class and give your own views
> - **read** views on what it is like to be a teenager

Big questions to find out what you know already.

> **Getting started**
>
> **Discuss this statement:**
>
> **"We are supposed to learn from adults, but I think they could learn a lot from us."**
>
> ***Yusef, 14 years old***

Important words for each unit. These words are included on wordlists in the Teacher's Resource.

> **depend** **look up to** **encourage** **help**

The key words feature includes vocabulary from other subjects.

> **Key words: Media studies**
>
> attitude
> headline
> impression

Read real texts with helpful glossaries.

> 16 empathy: the ability to imagine how other people feel
> 21 interdependence: helping each other
> 22 collaboration: working together
> 26 competitiveness: wanting to be better than other people
> 31 neurology: the study of the body's nervous system and how the brain works

Use of English boxes and accompanying questions present the main grammar points in a unit.

> **Use of English Present simple passive**
>
> Remember that we use the passive when we don't know who said or did something, or it isn't important who said or did it.
>
> ***We are told*** *that we behave worse than younger children.*
>
> *Defiant? It's when* ***you're asked*** *to do something, and you refuse.*

A brief revision of other language points.

> **Remember Compound nouns**
>
> A **compound noun** is usually a noun followed by another noun: *a beach umbrella, a car park.*
>
> Other types of compound noun include:
> - adjective + noun *hot springs*
> - verb ending in *-ing* + noun *a swimming pool*

Strategies you can use to help you with your learning.

Language tip

You can use ***do / does*** in positive sentences for emphasis:

*I **do** understand parents who want to limit screen time.*

Questions to help you think about how you learn.

- What do you have to think about when creating a timeline?
- Would you change anything on your timeline, now that you have compared it with the timelines of other groups?

This is what you have learned in the unit.

Summary checklist

I can

- [ ] describe the technology we will have in our homes in the future.
- [ ] take part in a discussion about social media and digital media.
- [ ] understand how archaeologists can use technology.
- [ ] make predictions of what life will be like in ten years' time.
- [ ] write a report on technology at school.
- [ ] read and understand extracts from a book about the history of science.

Questions that cover what you have learned in each unit. If you can answer these, you are ready to move on to the next unit.

Check your progress

General knowledge quiz

1 'Vlogging' is a combination of two words. What are the words, and what is 'vlogging'?

2 #

This symbol is used in music and it is sometimes used before numbers. What else is it used for?

Audio is available with the Digital Learner's Book, Teacher's Resource or Digital Classroom.

Video is available with Digital Classroom.

Lessons 1 and 4: The **Think about it** lessons introduce topic vocabulary.

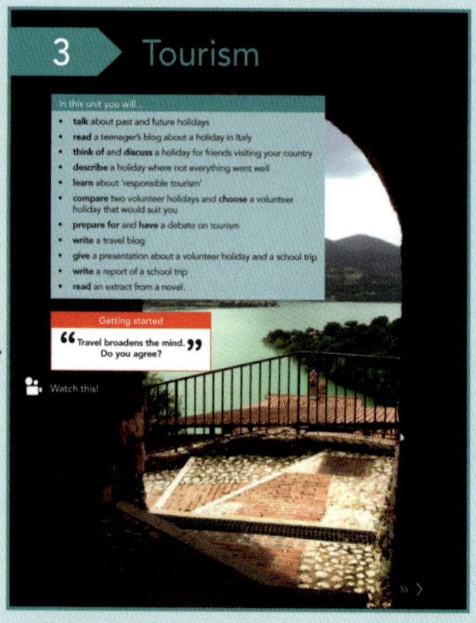

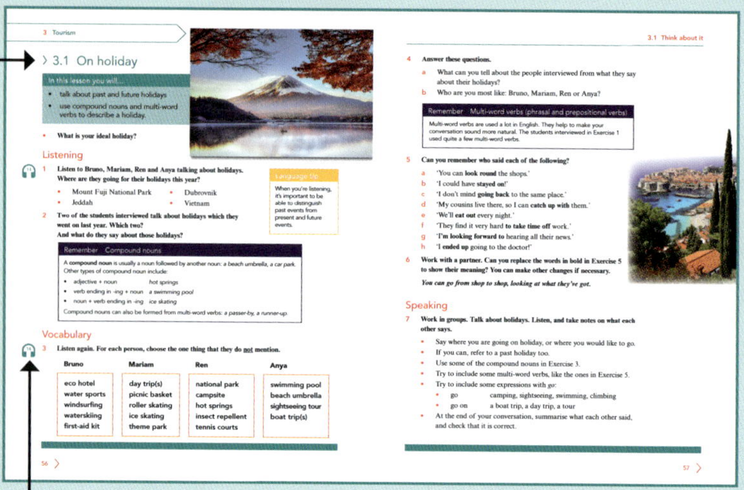

Engage with the topic of the unit and generate discussion using the image, the video and the big question.

These lessons include listening activities.

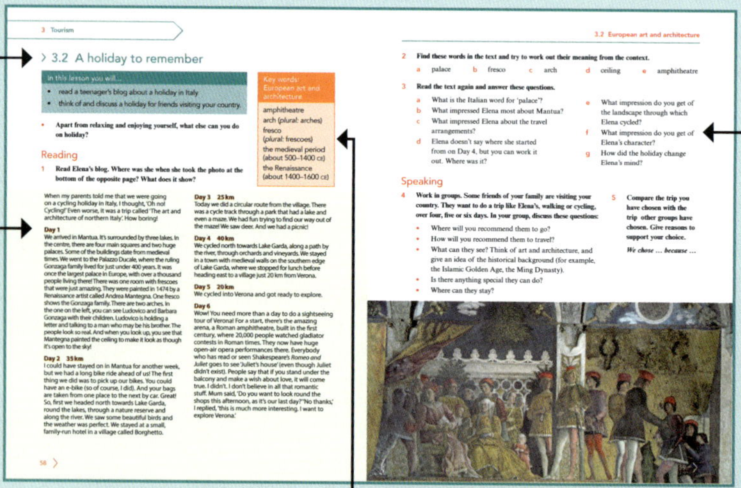

Lessons 2 and 5: The **cross-curricular** lessons prepare learners to learn in English across the curriculum.

There are opportunities to think critically about the information in the text.

A key text exposes learners to cross-curricular language.

In this lesson you'll find Key words boxes.

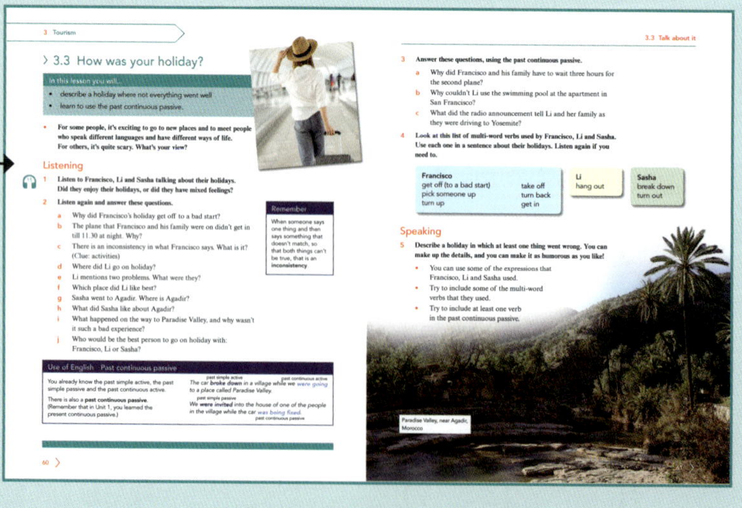

Lessons 3 and 6: The **Talk about it** lessons develop learners' speaking skills.

Listening models and speaking tips provide scaffolding for speaking.

Lesson 7:
The **Write about it** section supports learners in writing a variety of text types.

Model texts support the writing process.

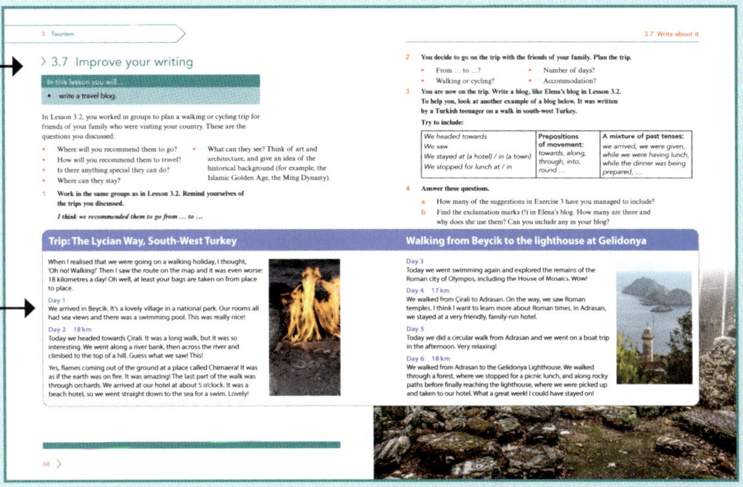

Step-by-step tasks support learners in their planning, writing and editing.

Assessment ideas and sample answers can be found in the Teacher's Resource.

Lesson 8:
The **Project challenge** lesson provides a choice of projects and an opportunity to consolidate learning from the unit.

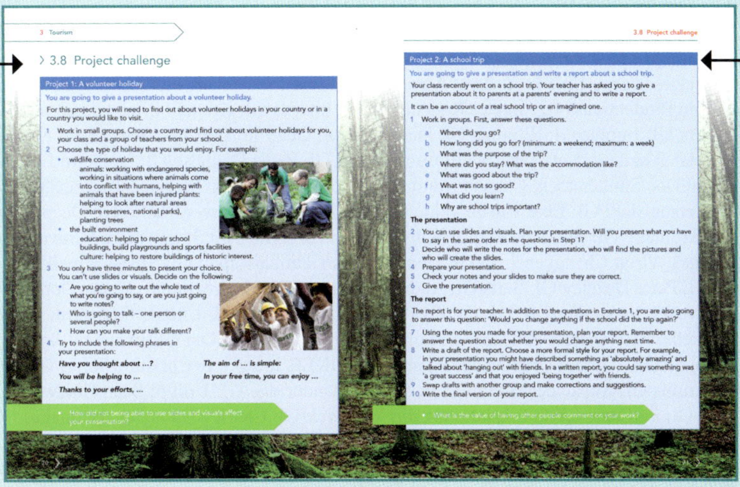

Projects encourage 21st-century skills such as research, collaboration and creativity.

Self- and peer-evaluation checklists for projects are available in the Teacher's Resource.

Lesson 9:
The **Read and respond** lesson is based on authentic texts and includes fiction, non-fiction, poetry and autobiography.

The audio can be played before learners read the text.

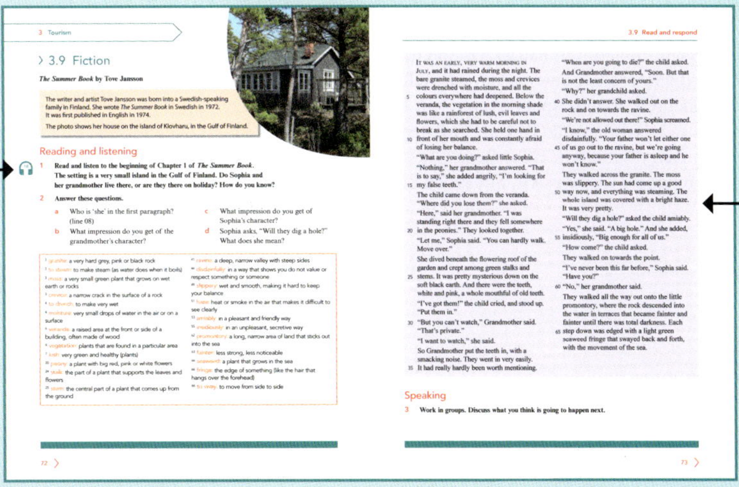

The literature is used as a platform for work on values.

There is also an opportunity for creative writing.

Acknowledgements

The authors and publishers would like to thank the following for reviewing this book: Tim Swihart, Mooltripakdee International School.

The authors and publishers acknowledge the following sources of copyright material and are grateful for the permissions granted. While every effort has been made, it has not always been possible to identify the sources of all the material used, or to trace all copyright holders. If any omissions are brought to our notice, we will be happy to include the appropriate acknowledgements on reprinting.

Unit 1: Behaviours graphic after Fred Zwicky, reproduced with permission; Extract from *My Name Is Tani ... and I Believe in Miracles* by Tanitoluwa Adewumi, Kayode Adewumi, Oluwatoyin Adewumi. Copyright © 2020 by Kayide Adewumi and Oluwatoyin Adewumi. Used by permission of Zondervan; **Unit 2:** 'Average person now spends more time on their phone and laptop than SLEEPING, study claims' by Madlen Davies. Adapted and reproduced with the permission of Solo Syndication; Extract from 'The Secret to Teenage Happiness (According To Science)' by Larissa Shashkof from https://www.1millionwomen.com.au/blog/. Reproduced with the permission of 1 Million Women; Extract abridged and adapted from *A Rainbow in Silk Stories from the Silk Road* by Cherry Gilchrist published by Barefoot Books. Reproduced with the permission of Barefoot Books; **Unit 3:** Extracts from *The Summer Book* by Tove Jansson use with the permission of R&B Licensing; **Unit 4:** 'Tortoise and Hare Race' © Jill Townsend 2000 Reproduced with permission; 'The Farmer's Cat' by David Greygoose adapted from a traditional Chinese story, translated by Xia Lu. Reproduced with the permission of The Windows Project Ward; **Unit 5:** Adapted from article 'Mediterranean shipwrecks reveal 'birth of globalisation' in trade' by Dalya Alberge. Copyright Guardian News & Media Ltd 2020. Reproduced with the permission of Guardian; Extracts from *A Little History of Science* by Professor William Bynum, 2012, Yale University Press. Reproduced with the permission of publisher; **Unit 6:** adapted extract from *The Lean and Happy Home* by Eva Jarlsdotter, published by Yellow Kite in 2019 (Hodder & Stoughton/Hachette). Reproduced with the permission of publisher and Nordlyset Agency (extract adapted and published by *The Daily Mail*); Extracts from *Humankind* by Rutget Bregman, reproduced with the permission of Bloomsbury Publishing and Hachette Group; **Unit 7:** RSPCA Young Photographer Award competition description from the RSPCA website, used with permission; Excerpt from *The Playbook: 52 Rules to Aim, Shoot, and Score in This Game Called Life by Kwame Alexander*. Copyright © 2017 by Kwame Alexander. Reprinted by permission of HarperCollins Publishers. All rights reserved; **Unit 8:** 'For Papatūānuku' by Nadine Ann Hura, reproduced with the permission of author; **Unit 9:** Graph 2 Sectoral aspirations in the UK, students aged 14/15 compared to those aged 17/18 from 'Disconnected: Career aspirations and jobs in the UK'. Reproduced with the permission of Education and Employers Charity; Excerpts from *Rickshaw Girl* Text copyright © 2007 by Mitali Perkins (Illustrations copyright © 2007 by Jamie Hogan) used with permission by Charlesbridge Publishing Inc., 9 Galen Street Suite 220, Watertown, MA 02474 (All rights reserved) and Listening Library, an imprint of Penguin Random House LLC. (All rights reserved).

Thanks to the following for permission to reproduce images:
Cover Barry Blackman/Corbis/Getty Images; *Inside* **Unit 1:** Abstract Aerial Art/GI; Jose Luis Pelaez Inc/GI; Kali9/GI; Kohei Hara/GI; Craig Barritt/GI; Oliver Rossi/GI; John P Kelly/GI; MoMo Productions/GI; Angeles Rodenas/SOPA Images/GI; Kristian Buus/GI; Losa5201/GI; FatCamera/GI; Cecilie_Arcurs/GI; Venkataramana Allam/EyeEm/GI; Bgblue/GI; Elfinima/GI; Dia Dipasupil/Getty Images for Tribeca Film Festival; Tamir Kalifa/GI; **Unit 2:** Robert Daly/GI; Rosemary Calvert/GI; GMVozd/GI; Karl Tapales/GI; Oscar Wong/GI; Paula Daniëlse/GI; Umberto Leporini / EyeEm/GI; CREATISTA/Shutterstock; PathDoc/Shutterstock; PathDoc/Shutterstock; Chepko Danil Vitalevich/Shutterstock; Suzanne Tucker/Shutterstock; ProStockStudio/Shutterstock; PathDoc/Shutterstock; RyersonClark/GI; Elke Van de Velde/GI; Ron Levine/GI; Yasser Chalid/GI; Deepak Sethi/GI; Slonov/GI; Carol Yepes/GI; Marrio31/GI; CSA-Archive/GI; Mikroman6/GI; Ben Pipe Photography/GI; GMVozd/GI; **Unit 3:** Salvatore Varavallo/GI; DoctorEgg/GI; Vladimir zakharov/GI; Art Images via Getty Images; Virojt Changyencham/GI; Gerard Sioen/Gamma-Rapho/GI; Elisa Cicinelli/GI; Neil Overy/GI; Merrill Images/GI; Chris Minihane/GI; Anton Petrus/GI; Peter Dazeley/GI; Serts/GI; Andrey Nekrasov/GI; okanmetin/GI; Ozgur Donmaz/GI; Jose Luis Pelaez Inc/GI; Jose Luis Pelaez Inc/GI; Tomasz Bobrzynski (tomanthony)/GI; Jeff Gilbert/Alamy; okanmetin/GI; **Unit 4:** Caracterdesign/GI; Jhillphotography/GI; Marco Bottigelli/GI; Traveler1116/GI; Ariel Skelley/GI; Andrew Brookes/GI; SolStock/GI; Jason J Mulikita/GI; Image by Jay Schipper/GI; Shene/GI; seng chye teo/GI; Photo by Steve Stone/GI; Manoj Shah/GI; Grant Ordelheide/GI; imageBROKER/Juergen & Christine Sohns/GI; Sciepro/Science Photo Library/GI; Bernd Von Jutrczenka/Pool/GI; Pukrufus/GI; Alexander Grumeth/GI; Sandra Standbridge/GI; **Unit 5:** Sean Gladwell/GI; Pixelfit/GI; Peter Dazeley/GI; Piranka/GI; Baona/GI; PressureUA/GI; FatCamera/GI; Tagphoto/GI; Jirí Václavek/GI; Charley Gallay/Getty Images for Gray Malin; Os Tartarouchos/GI; Narvikk/GI; © Enigma Recoveries UK; © Enigma Recoveries UK; Hakule/GI; SolStock/GI; Metamorworks/GI; Chesky_W/GI; Yuichiro Chino/GI; Aaaaimages/GI; Fotosearch/GI; Carl Court/GI; Miakievy/GI; Sjoerd van der Wal/GI; DeAgostini/GI; CM Dixon/Print Collector/GI; Werner Forman/GI; Fotosearch/GI; CPA Media Pte Ltd/Alamy; Gideon Mendel/GI; **Unit 6:** Bloomimage/GI; metamorworks/GI; Uwe Krejci/GI; Kate_sept2004/GI; Jose Luis Pelaez Inc/GI; Tetra Images/GI; Skynesher/GI; Eastnine Inc/GI; JGI/GI; Chris Ryan/GI; Philippe Turpin/GI; SDI Productions/GI; Frédéric Soltan/Corbis via Getty Images; Andrew Brookes/GI; Maskot/GI; Simone Padovani/GI; Alexis Rosenfeld/GI; Holger Leue/GI; Jeff Pachoud/GI; **Unit 7:** Tim de Waele/GI MananVatsyayana/GI; Geber86/GI; Adek Berry/GI; Aamir Qureshi/GI; Kohei Hara/GI; Ward Williams Films/GI; Yuri Smityuk/GI; Rafe Swan/GI; Floortje/GI; Htu/GI; Gary Yeowell/GI; Westend61/GI; Maja Hitij/GI; Chaiwat Subprasom/Pacific Press/GI; GaudiLab/GI; Romilly Lockyer/GI; 24K-Production/GI; Matthias Hangst/Bongarts/GI; Yasuyoshi Chiba/GI; David Charles Bishop/GI; Zhangshuang/GI; Slaven Vlasic/GI; Bettmann/GI; Phoenixns/GI; **Unit 8:** Hiroshi Watanabe/GI; Adastra/GI; imagedepotpro/GI; Patrick Orton/GI; Chase Dekker Wild-Life Images/GI; HollyHarry/Shutterstock; Yulkapopkova/GI; Anchiy/GI; Iryna Mylinska/GI; Natalie Board/GI; Larissa Veronesi/GI; Seramo/GI; MirageC/GI; Mike Harrington/GI; AzmanL/GI; Ronaldo Schemidt/GI; E4C/GI; David Tipling/GI; Kristianbell/GI; RenataAphotography/GI; Dougal Waters/GI; Dynasoar/GI; Sunisa Kanphian/GI; Mlenny/GI; irmaferreira/GI; Culture Club/GI; Jakkapan Jabjainai/GI; Kristianbell/GI; **Unit 9:** Artpartner-images/GI; Sdi Productions/GI; Efren Landaos/Sopa Images/GI; by kind permission of Vitoria Mario; Izusek/GI; Gerry Smith/GI; Clive Rose/GI; © UNHCR/Benjamin Loyseau; DrAfter123/GI; Dpa picture alliance/Alamy; Jim Newberry/Alamy; John Lamparski/GI; Jonathan Knowles/GI; Sdi Productions/GI; Gards/GI; Terry Vine/GI; Anand purohit/GI; Amit Basu Photography/GI; Sourav Saha Photography/GI

Key: GI = Getty Images

1 Views and voices

In this unit you will…

- **listen to** views on talking in class and give your own views
- **read** views on what it is like to be a teenager
- **discuss** what you would expect to find in a book about teenage psychology
- **listen to** students talking about role models and give your own views
- **listen to** a conversation about stereotypes of teenagers and give your own views
- **read** and compare two reports of the same event
- **discuss** how and why reports of the same event can be different
- **learn** about what makes a good presentation
- **write** an email to a student in another country asking about teenage life there
- **learn** to interpret a photo
- **give** a presentation on teenage life
- **read** extracts from an autobiography.

Getting started

Discuss this statement:

“We are supposed to learn from adults, but I think they could learn a lot from us.”

Yusef, 14 years old

Watch this!

1.1 What helps you to learn?

In this lesson you will…

- listen to students' views on talking in class
- give your views on talking in class
- revise and use *-ing* forms.

- **Do you like working in groups or do you prefer working on your own? Are there times when it's good to talk in a lesson?**

Eva Tarak Anna Joseph Han Milo

Listening

02

1 **Listen to this interview between a journalist and six students: Eva, Tarak, Anna, Joseph, Han and Milo. What do the students think about talking in class? Who is for it? Who is against it? Who has mixed feelings?**

Vocabulary

2 **Choose the correct meaning of the words and phrases in bold. To help you, you can listen again.**

a If you **interrupt** someone while they are speaking, you *tell them to be quiet / speak while they are speaking*.

b If you **compare** two things, you *look at the ways they are similar or different / add them together*.

c If you **distract** someone, you *take their attention away from something / upset them*.

d If you **encourage** someone to do something, you *want them to believe they can do something / want them to be careful about doing something*.

e If you **tell someone off**, you *tell them to go away / speak angrily to them because they have done something wrong*.

f If you **get into trouble for** doing something, you *are worried about something / are in a situation where you have done something wrong*.

g If you **share** ideas, you *let other people know what they are / keep them secret*.

h If you **are supposed to** do something, *people expect you to do it / you're ready to do it*.

i If you **concentrate on** something, you *give it all your attention / are puzzled by it*.

02

3 **Listen again. Use the verbs in bold in Exercise 2 in the correct form to complete the journalist's notes.**

Eva: Often asks a classmate instead of interrupting the teacher.

Tarak: Says that you can learn by ________ answers.

Anna: Says that talking in class ________ you from getting on with your work.

Joseph: Teachers ________ students to talk quietly during the lesson, if it's about work.

Han: Teachers sometimes ________ students ________ for talking in class. Han ________ ________ trouble for chatting to her friends.

Milo: ________ ideas helps him to learn. Sometimes people talk when they're not ________ to, so you can't ________ ________ what you're doing.

Use of English -ing forms

Remember that we use *-ing* forms after certain verbs:

Our teachers ***don't mind*** *us* ***talking*** *quietly.*

We use *-ing* forms after prepositions:

I sometimes get into trouble ***for chatting*** *in class.*

We can also use *-ing* forms as the subject of a verb:

Sharing *ideas helps me to learn.*

Speaking

4 **What do you think about talking in class? Work in groups and share your views.**

I agree with Milo. Sharing ideas helps me to learn. But I'm also a bit like Han, because I sometimes get into trouble for chatting with my friends.

Speaking tip

Be careful to use *-ing* forms in the correct places. If you make a mistake when you are speaking, just stop and correct it.

I sometimes get into trouble for chat with my … I mean, for chatting with … my friends.

Writing

5 **Here is the beginning of a magazine article that the journalist wrote after interviewing the students. Use the notes in Exercise 3 and your own ideas to complete it.**

You might get into trouble for chatting in class, but education experts have found that talking to your classmates can be helpful. 'Students should be encouraged to explain things to each other and to discuss things,' they say.

I talked to some students to find out what they thought about talking in class. For some of them, talking in class is a good thing, because …

1.2 Teenage psychology

In this lesson you will...

- read views on what it is like to be a teenager
- discuss what you would expect to find in a book about teenage psychology.

- **How do teenagers think and act differently from adults?**

Reading

1 **Read the extracts. Which do you think were written by teenagers? Which were written by parents of teenagers? Which one was written by a psychologist?**

a I think they should give us a bit more freedom and understanding. We need to feel independent and grown up, because we are in the process of becoming adults. And give us time, listen to us, talk to us, tell us what's going on in your life!

b I often think they're right and I'm wrong. They just see the world differently. And after all, I was like them once.

c You're always trying to find the balance between keeping them safe and letting them go. In my experience, we are not good at 'risk assessment'. For example, they want to go to a music festival and you don't sleep because you're terrified that they are going to get into all sorts of trouble. They go, they come back, and they've had a great time. They want to go on a cycle ride in the country with a couple of friends, and you're very happy. They go, they come back, but one of them nearly had an accident when a car came too close.

d I don't mind them telling me off when I do something wrong, but I wish they wouldn't go on about it. Yes, I've made a mistake, I shouldn't have done it, I'm sorry, now let's move on.

e Most of the scientific evidence shows that today's teenagers are more sensible than their parents were at that age. Brain scans of teenagers show that by the end of the second decade of life, teenagers have developed formidable powers of problem-solving, creativity, self-analysis, focus, ambition, communication and social flexibility. Twenty-year-olds are better than ten-year-olds at everything.

f There are a lot of negative stereotypes about us – that we're lazy, we only think about ourselves, we just want to have a good time. But most of my friends work hard and want to do well.

2 **Work in pairs. What do the following words mean? You may be able to work out the meaning from the context. For example:**

In extract e, the word 'formidable' appears. What sort of word is it?

(*It's an adjective. It describes 'powers'.*)

Is the writer saying that these powers are good or bad, strong or weak?

(*Good, strong – very good, very strong.*)

'Formidable' means 'great, very impressive, demanding respect'.

If you can't work out the meaning from the context, find the word in a dictionary.

Key words: Psychology

ambition: ideas about what you want to do in the future
communication: talking or writing to other people
creativity: using your imagination to express yourself in art, writing, music, etc.
focus: the ability to concentrate on something
problem-solving: finding the answer to a difficult question or situation
self-analysis: understanding yourself
social flexibility: being able to get on with all sorts of people

a grown up
b risk assessment
c terrified
d evidence
e sensible
f brain scan
g decade
h stereotype

Speaking

3 **Work with a partner. Ask and answer these questions, giving examples to support your answers.**

a Are you good at problem-solving?
Yes, I'm quite good. I like doing word puzzles and number puzzles.

b Are you creative?

c Are you able to analyse yourself? Can you always give reasons for the things you do and the way you feel?

d Are you good at focussing on something, concentrating on it for a period of time?

e Are you ambitious?

f Are you a good communicator?

g Are you able to get on with all sorts of people?

4 **Work in groups. The psychologist whose words were quoted in Exercise 1 wrote a book about teenagers. If you were advising him about what to include in the book, what would you say? Discuss:**

- your relationships with friends and family
- daily routine (school, free time, sleep …)
- the way you feel.

Student A: *People don't understand that being a teenager can be difficult. You want to feel independent and grown up, but in your parents' eyes you are still a child.*
Student B: *I think there's a big difference between being 13 and being 19.*
Student C: *What do you mean?*
Student B: *When you're 13, 14, 15, you're changing really quickly. By the time you're 19, you're an adult.*

1.3 Role models

In this lesson you will...

- listen to students talking about role models and give your own views
- revise and use the present simple and continuous.

- **What is a role model?**

Listening

03

1 **Listen to this conversation between Theo, Mai and Leila. What is it about?**

2 **Answer these questions.**

a What are Leila and Mai doing at the beginning of the conversation, when Theo says hello to them?

b The magazine article says that teenagers are obsessed by celebrities and all look up to them as role models. Leila says, 'That's just a stereotype.' What does she mean?

c The person in the second photo is Marley Dias. Who are the people in the other photos?

d Mai, Leila and Theo give examples of people who are role models for them. What can you remember about them?

e Theo and Leila each say something that suggests they too have stereotypes. What are they?

f All three agree about one thing. What is it?

Use of English Present simple and present continuous

Present simple

Positive	Negative	Question
I play volleyball. She plays tennis.	I don't play basketball. She doesn't play badminton.	What do you play? What does he play?

Present continuous

Positive	Negative	Question
I'm reading a book at the moment.	I'm not listening to music.	What are you doing?

Use of English Present simple and present continuous

We use the present continuous for things happening at the moment:

What are you reading?

We also use it for temporary situations:

You aren't watching the ball.

This means that this is not what usually happens: you usually watch the ball but in this practice session, you aren't watching it, and this is causing problems.

And we can use the present continuous for fixed arrangements:

She's going to a tennis camp this summer.

There is an unusual use of the present continuous with *always*:

He's always helping other people.

This means that he helps people more than you would expect, more than is normal.

3 **Choose the present simple or the present continuous of these verbs to complete the sentences.**

depend	look up to	encourage	help	save up for

a At the moment, he ***'s helping*** children who have problems with their reading.

b They say we all .... celebrities as role models.

c It .... what they're famous for.

d I .... the trip to the tennis camp.

e He's good because he .... me to believe in myself.

Speaking

4 **Work in groups. Discuss these three questions.**

a Think of five famous people – celebrities – in the world of music, sport or the arts. Are they good role models? Give your reasons.

b Who are your role models? Why are they good role models for you?

c Is it better to have role models who are similar in age to you, or ones who are older than you?

In your discussion, try to include the verbs in Exercise 3, the phrases in the Speaking tip and some of the following words and phrases:

(teenagers) are obsessed by celebrities
a stereotype
be supposed to
ambition
one of the most influential

Speaking tip

Anyway is a useful word when you want to change the direction of the conversation, or to go back to an earlier point in the conversation. This is what Mai does in the conversation in Exercise 1: *Anyway, Theo, what about you?*

It's just that … is a good way of explaining or justifying something you've said: *It's just that he encourages me to believe in myself.*

1.4 Teenage voices

In this lesson you will...

- listen to a conversation about stereotypes of teenagers and give your own views
- revise and use the present simple passive.

- **What are the stereotypes of teenagers?**

Reading

1 **Read the following introduction to an article describing a study carried out in Chinese middle schools. What do you think the purpose of the study was?**

> In many societies, teenagers are repeatedly told – by adults, peers and popular media – that teens are more likely than younger children to take risks, ignore their parents, skip schoolwork and succumb to bad influences. But stereotypes are not destiny, a new study of Chinese middle school students suggests.

2 **Answer these questions.**

a Does the first sentence say that generally people think teenagers behave better or worse than younger children?

b If someone 'skips schoolwork', do they do their schoolwork or not?

c If someone 'succumbs to bad influences', are they more likely to do bad things or good things?

d The writer says, 'stereotypes are not destiny'. How could you say this in other words?

e Look at the last sentence of the text. What does it tell you about the conclusion of the study?

Listening and vocabulary

04

3 **Listen to the conversation and look at the word clouds. What do they show?**

4 **Work with a partner. Look at the words in the word clouds. Say what they mean, using examples to illustrate the meaning.**

Student A: *'Rebellious' – that's when you don't do what you're told to do, isn't it?*

Student B: *Yes. People think all teenagers are rebellious, because they don't always follow the rules.*

Student A: *What about 'disrespectful'?*

> **Use of English** Present simple passive
>
> Remember that we use the passive when we don't know who said or did something, or it isn't important who said or did it.
>
> ***We are told*** *that we behave worse than younger children.*
>
> *Defiant? It's when* ***you're asked*** *to do something, and you refuse.*

5 **Complete these sentences to make them true for you and your friends.**

- **a** I'm (often) told that I'm …
- **b** We are (sometimes) told that …
- **c** We are thought to be …
- **d** I'm / We are expected to …
- **e** I'm not / We aren't expected to …

Speaking

6 **Work with a partner or in groups. Say whether you think the words in the word clouds apply to you and teenagers you know. Use the conversation in Exercise 3 as a model and try to include some sentences from Exercise 5.**

1.5 Facts and opinions

In this lesson you will...

- read two reports of the same event and compare them
- discuss how and why reports of the same event can be different.

Key words: Media studies

attitude
headline
impression

- **When you read or hear a news story, can you sometimes tell what the attitude and opinions of the reporter are?**

Reading

1 **Read this news report. What impression do you get of what happened?**

TODAY

Teenage rage

THOUSANDS OF TEENAGERS went on strike from school and descended on Parliament Square in central London yesterday. It was Friday, the last day of the school week, and a lovely sunny day.

In the UK as a whole, there were almost 200 demos by school-age students. They were on strike to protest about climate change.

This time of year is particularly important for 16- and 18-year-olds, as exams are just starting to take place in schools around the country. However, for the protestors, the issue of climate change was clearly more important than exam preparation.

They marched from Parliament Square to the Department for Education, shouting

and carrying placards with strongly worded messages.

The march made life very difficult for ordinary people who work in the area and for tourists enjoying the sights of London.

One defiant young protester held up a rather tired-looking toy monkey that had a label round its neck saying, 'Wake up humans, you're endangered too'.

By the end of the day, the cafés were full and central London returned to normal. All that was left was a lot of litter.

rage: extreme anger that you can't control

[1] go on strike: stop working for a period of time as a protest

[2] descend: *(formal)* go down

[7] demo: short for 'demonstration', an event where people walk or stand together to show they have a strong opinion about something

[12] issue: an important subject or problem

[17] placard: a large piece of card with a message on it

2 **Read the second article. What impression do you get of the journalist who wrote it?**

THE EXAMINER

Take climate change seriously, say school students

Yesterday, in London and other UK cities, 150 demonstrations took place to ask politicians to take the issue of climate change seriously. School students from all over the country felt strongly enough to take a day off from exam preparation to protest. They carried placards saying, 'It's our future' and 'I'd be at school if the Earth was cool!'

The march from Parliament Square to the Department for Education was peaceful. Protestors were respectful of those who were not part of the march. At the Department for Education, protestors handed in a petition with the title 'Teach the future', asking the education minister to include lessons on climate change in the school curriculum.

Although there was a heavy police presence, the atmosphere was calm. The day ended at 8 p.m. 'It's been an important day,' said Alicia, one of the protestors. 'Anyway, I'm going home now to revise for my history exam on Monday.'

[15] petition: a document with a lot of people's names on it, that asks someone in authority to do something

Speaking

3 **Compare the two accounts and discuss them. Think about:**

- the headline (the title of the article)
- the choice of photos
- the choice of words
- the details and examples given
- the impression of teenagers you get from each article.

Writing

4 **Based on the discussion you had, write a paragraph about the differences between the articles.**

1.6 From ideas into words

In this lesson you will...

- learn about and discuss what makes a good presentation
- revise and use the present continuous passive.

- **How do you feel about giving presentations in class?**

Reading

1 **Read the rules on giving presentations. Match the paragraph headings with paragraphs a–h.**

Paragraph headings

Make it visual
Timing is important
Practice makes perfect
Get it right
Don't put too much text on a slide
Involve your audience right from the start
Don't be nervous about the audience interrupting you
Plan your presentation carefully

Rules for giving a presentation, using presentation software

a It gives a very bad impression if there are mistakes on your slides, so check your spelling, punctuation and grammar.

b Rehearse your presentation carefully. Speak clearly and slowly. Think of yourselves as actors in a theatre.

c After the title slide, you'll show a slide with text, or a picture or both. Use this slide to ask a question.

d The audience must be able to read the text on your slides easily. In most cases, four lines of text per slide is enough.

e There's a saying, 'A picture is worth a thousand words.' Think about it!

f You need a clear idea of the structure of your presentation before you decide on the text and pictures.

g Time your presentation and note down the time when each new slide should appear.

h The audience will feel more engaged if they are allowed to make comments and ask questions during your presentation.

Listening

05

2 **Listen to some students preparing a presentation. They mention three of the rules in Exercise 1. Which three?**

3 **Listen again. Answer these questions.**

a What is the presentation about?

b What equipment are the students going to use?

c What will the audience see after the title slide?

d What might appear on the placards?

e What are the students going to do first?

Use of English Present continuous passive

We use the present continuous passive when we don't know who is doing something, or it isn't important:

(The audience need to feel that) *they* ***are being entertained***.

The focus is on the audience here, not on the people doing the presentation.

Complete the answers to these questions, using the present continuous passive.

Q: Why can't the students go into the art room at the moment?

A: Because the art room .... for an exhibition.

Q: What's happening on the first slide of the presentation?

A: Some teenagers .... questions about teenage life by a TV journalist.

4 **Use the present continuous passive to make the prompts in italics into full sentences.**

a There's a lot of building work going on at our school.
A new drama studio / build
A new drama studio is being built.

b We can't we go into the school hall. *It / clean*

c I'm nervous about the interview we did with the TV journalist.
It / show / on TV this evening!

d The canteen is closed today. *Drinks and snacks / serve / in the small hall.*

e Don't look round. *We / follow / by your cat!*

Speaking

5 **You are going to give a presentation on teenage life. Discuss how you are going to prepare for it. Start like this:**

So we've got to do a presentation on teenage life …

What shall we do first?

You will have a chance to give this presentation in Project 2 in Lesson 1.8.

Speaking tip

Making suggestions

We could …

Let's …

Why don't we …?

Shall we …?

1.7 Improve your writing

In this lesson you will...

- write an email to a friend.

1 **Work in pairs. Read the email on the opposite page and answer these questions.**

a Who is Lily and what do we know about her?

b What do we know about Céline?

c Why is Céline writing to Lily?

d If Céline asked you the questions in her email, how would you answer them?

e How would you describe the tone of the email: formal, informal, friendly, businesslike ...?

2 **You are doing a project at school on teenage life. Write an email to a penfriend in another country, similar to Céline's, asking about teenage life in your friend's country. Follow this plan. You can use as many of the phrases from Céline's email as you like.**

> Dear ...
>
> I hope ... . It's been a long time since we have been in touch. I often wonder how you are and what you are doing. I'm ...
>
> Anyway, the reason I'm writing is ...
>
> ... . So I wonder if you could help me by answering these questions:
>
> 1 *Ask about stereotypes*
>
> 2 *Ask about the media*
>
> 3 *Ask about role models*
>
> *Thank them for their help*
>
> Looking forward ...

New Message

From: Céline

To: Lily   **Cc** **Bcc**

Dear Lily,

I hope you and your family are well. It's been a long time since we have been in touch. I often wonder how you are and what you are doing. I'm so busy with my grandchildren and my studies that I don't have much time to myself! Are you still doing your art classes?

Anyway, the reason I'm writing is to ask you for some help with something I'm doing for my creative writing course at the moment. We're writing a short story about what it's like to be someone of our age. I thought it would be good if we could do something about older people in other countries: how they see themselves and how they are seen by younger people. Perhaps it's the same all over the world, but I don't know and I'd like to find out. So I wonder if you could help me by answering these questions:

1. Are there stereotypes of older people in your country? What sort of words do young people use to describe older people? Are they mostly negative or positive?
2. How are older people shown in the media? Are there TV programmes about older people, for example? What do they show?
3. Do you or your friends still have a role model or role models? Are any of them younger people? Why are they role models?

I'd really appreciate your help with this, so thank you in advance!

Looking forward to hearing from you.

Céline

Send

1.8 Project challenge

Project 1: Interpreting a photo

You are going to write an account of a photo. You can work individually or with a partner.

1 First, write notes about this photo in answer to these questions, but do not share your notes with other students.

a Who are the boys in the photo?
b Where are they?
c What are they doing?
d What time of day is it?
e What has just happened?
f Who is the boy on the right phoning? / Who is phoning the boy?
g What is going to happen?

2 Write your account, based on the answers to the questions in Exercise 1.

The boys in the photo are friends: Krishna, on the left, and Bimal. They're in a park ...

3 Compare your account with the accounts of other students. What does the comparison show you?

The way I see it, the boys are ...

That's not how I see it at all. To me, they're ...

- What did you learn from doing this project?

Project 2: A ten-minute presentation on teenage life

You are going to prepare and give a presentation on teenage life. Work in groups.

1 Plan your presentation. Here is an idea for a presentation in five sections:

1	Stereotypes	Positive or negative?	
2	The teenage brain	Is it different?	
3	Life at school	In the classroom	Outside the classroom
4	Role models	Who are they?	Are they important?
5	Conclusion and questions		

2 How are you going to work?

Shall we all plan the presentation together?

Karib and Adam, could you make notes on what should go on each slide?

Imane, you're good at Art and Design. Could you choose the visuals and create the slides?

Let's write the script together.

Do we need a complete script or just notes?

OK, to summarise: we'll plan the presentation together. Then Karib and Adam will …

3 Write a draft and prepare your slides

4 Check the slides and the notes / script.

- Are the slides clear (not too much text)?
- Have you checked the grammar, spelling and punctuation?

5 Rehearse your presentation.

- Are you going to read from a script or use notes?
- Were your timings correct? Did you finish in ten minutes?

6 Decide if you need to make any changes.

7 Give your presentation.

- What have you learned from giving this presentation?

1.9 Autobiography

My Name is Tani is by Tanitoluwa Adewumi. The subtitle of the book is 'The amazing true story of one boy's journey from refugee to chess champion'.

Tani and his family had to leave their home in Abuja, the capital of Nigeria, and seek asylum in America. At first, they stayed with relatives in Dallas. Then they went to New York and lived in a shelter for homeless people in Manhattan. (Tani calls the shelter the 'Hotel' in his book.) Tani's father, who had been a successful businessman in Nigeria, worked as a taxi driver and in a restaurant kitchen, washing dishes. His mother, an accountant by profession, worked as a cleaner.

Tani started at an elementary school in New York. It was there that one of the teachers, Shawn Martinez, introduced Tani to chess. He loved the game and learned quickly. At the age of eight, he took part in the New York State Championship for third-grade children and won. Tani's coaches raised money through crowdfunding to provide a place for the family to live, so Tani played his part in helping the family to settle into a new life.

06

1 **Read and listen to the first extract from *My Name is Tani*. At this point, Tani is eight years old. Austin is his older brother. What impression do you get of Tani?**

2 **Work with a partner. Find these phrases in the text and try to work out what they mean from the context.**

- a that was funny, but not in a rude way (line 15)
- b some kids were messing around (line 24)
- c but I nodded anyway (line 29)
- d I'm grateful for that (line 43)
- e she doesn't … make a big deal out of it (line 46)

3 **Tani describes his feelings about his mum in an unusual way:**

I like that she cooks good food. (line 36)

I like that she corrects me. (line 41)

I like that she helps me with my chess. (line 44)

He could have said:

I like the food she cooks.

I like it when she corrects me.

I like it when she helps me with my chess.

Why do you think Tani chooses to say 'I like that she …' each time?

4 **Work in groups. Discuss these questions.**

- a How would you describe the relationship between Tani, his brother Austin and their mum and dad?
- b If someone asked you the question 'What do you like about them?' about an adult in your life, what would you say?

My Name is Tani

One day while we were walking to the basketball court, Austin and I talked about Mum and Dad.

I said, 'What do you most like about them?'

Austin started talking about Dad and said, 'He's hardworking and wants the best for us, and he's always reminding us to focus and pay attention and become great people in life.'

I said, 'I like all those things too.'

Then Austin said, 'Wait, I forgot. I have one more thing to add about Dad. I like his suits.'

That was funny, but not in a rude way, because Dad really does have a lot of suits, and all of them look really good.

Then I said, 'What about Mum?'

Austin thought for a moment. He said, 'She's the best at teaching moral lessons, and she's always trying to guide us away from bad things. Did you know the other day when I was on a school trip, some kids were messing around badly, but I made them stop because I remembered all those stories she'd told us about how important school is?

(Austin had already told me that story about the school trip, but I nodded anyway.)

We reached the court then, and it was time to play, so *I* didn't get to say what I like most about Mum. But all the time we were playing, I was thinking about her and what my answer would be.

I like that she cooks good food. She can make anything taste good, and all the time we were living at the Hotel, I think she really missed not having a kitchen of her own.

I like that she corrects me. Well, maybe I don't like it, but I know that it's helpful, so I'm grateful for that.

Most of all, I like that she helps me with my chess. When I don't play well, she doesn't get angry or make a big deal out of it like some parents do. She just says, 'Do you think you can do better?' And I say yes, and she says, 'Well, if you work hard and concentrate and do your very best, that will be good enough.' And she takes me to chess tournaments. She's never too busy, even though she also takes Austin to his basketball games and cooks all the time and has her own job too.

07

5 **Read and listen to the second extract from *My Name is Tani*. What is Tani's attitude towards Coach Shawn?**

Next, Coach Shawn started talking about chess, and I listened hard. I even moved places so I could be right in the front row and able to see him up close. I wanted to make sure I heard every word he said.

'We've been working here for three months now, and I know you all know the moves of the pieces, but I've got to tell you that knowing the moves is not enough. The concept of the game is a lot deeper. If you want to be good at chess, you've got to learn how to make good decisions.'

Then he said something strange. 'Raise your hand if you know how to cross the street.'

I put my hand up in the air. I looked around and everyone else had too.

Coach Shawn nodded. Then he said, 'Right. Is it simple or difficult to cross the street?'

We all called out, 'It's simple!'

'Okay, but if one day you forget what to do when you're crossing the street, and you forget to look both ways and make that mistake, what could happen to you?'

I had my hand up high. Mum had been talking to me a lot about crossing the street ever since we'd moved to the Hotel, because the roads in New York are a lot busier than they are in Dallas or most places in Nigeria. When Coach Shawn called on me to answer, I said, 'You'd be hit by a car, and you might die.'

He said, 'Yes, that's right, Tani. Even a simple thing like crossing the street can have really bad consequences for your life. And that's like chess. You might think that since you're just making a simple move you can make it fast and not think about it carefully, but you can end up in so much trouble. You've got to think the consequences through. You've got to think deep. Otherwise you're going to end up in trouble.'

I liked everything that Coach Shawn said. Everything.

That's when I knew that I really wanted to be a chess player.

6 **Answer these questions.**

- **a** Coach Shawn says, 'Raise your hand if you know how to cross the street.' Why do you think Tani finds this strange?
- **b** Coach Shawn wants to make sure the young chess players understand a very important point about the game. What is it?
- **c** What is the conclusion he draws from the example of crossing the street?
- **d** What impression does this lesson leave on Tani?
- **e** Tani ends by saying, 'That's when I knew that I really wanted to be a chess player.' What has made him come to this decision?

7 **Choose one of the following:**

- Look again at the last three paragraphs of the extract on the previous page. Write a similar appreciation of someone you know.
- Read the second extract again. Write an appreciation of a particular lesson you have learned from a teacher or someone like Coach Shawn.

Check your progress

General knowledge quiz

1 How many years is a decade?

2 What is a stereotype?

3 What does a journalist do?

4 What is a brain scan?

5 What is a role model?

6 What is a word cloud?

7 'Demo' is short for a longer word. What is that word?

8 It's a document with a lot of people's names on it. It asks someone in authority to do something. It can be a paper document or it can be online. What is it?

9 If you go on strike, what do you do?

10 Complete this saying: 'A picture is worth a thousand …'

Vocabulary

Classroom interaction

1 **Use the words in the box in the correct form to complete the sentences.**

chat	compare	distract
encourage	interrupt	share

a Our classroom is next to the music room, so when students are having piano or violin lessons, it sometimes ***distracts*** you from your work.

b Please don't .... the teacher while she's explaining what you need to do. Save your questions until the end.

c In science, we're .... different kinds of metal, and matching them to their uses.

d We enjoy working in groups because .... ideas helps you to learn.

e Our games teacher .... us to try all kinds of sport, to find one that suits us.

f It's OK to talk about the work you're doing, but our teachers don't like us .... about other things.

2 **What are the missing words in these sentences?**

a It's hard to get ***on*** with your homework when the TV is on.

b I'm doing quite well at school, although I sometimes get .... trouble for being late.

c Our teachers tell us .... for running in the corridors.

d You're supposed .... leave your mobile phones at Reception.

Use of English

1 **Complete the second sentence so that it means the same as the first.**

- **a** I swim, but not in the sea.
  I don't like ***swimming in the sea***.
- **b** It's OK with me if we have a pizza.
  I don't mind …………
- **c** I'm not going to eat chocolate every day.
  I'm going to stop …………
- **d** I'm pleased you came to see me. Thank you.
  Thank you for …………

2 **Choose the correct option in each of these dialogues.**

- **a** **A:** I think we should be able to use dictionaries in exams.
  B: I ***'m agreeing / agree*** with you.
- **b** **A:** Where's Orlando?
  B: He ***'s talking / talks*** to Mr Lin.
- **c** **A:** Would you like to come to my house after school?
  B: Sorry, I ***'m having / have*** swimming practice every Wednesday evening.
- **d** **A:** Here's your tea. Now, where's the sugar?
  B: It's OK. I ***'m not taking / don't take*** sugar.
- **e** **A:** Are there any questions about plans for this term?
  B: ***Do we go / Are we going*** on a school trip?

3 **Rewrite these sentences using the present simple passive.**

- **a** People tell me that I'm a bit loud sometimes.
  I'm told that I'm a bit loud sometimes.
- **b** My parents expect me to tidy my room every Saturday.
- **c** Our school encourages us to play a musical instrument.
- **d** We invite all parents to come to the end-of-term concert.

4 **Answer these questions. Use *because* and the verb in brackets in the present continuous passive.**

- **a** Why can't we go into the drama studio? *(repaint)*
  Because it's being repainted.
- **b** Why can't we go into the gym? *(clean)*
- **c** Why can't I use the computer? *(repair)*
- **d** Why are you taking those letters to the office? *(send / to parents this afternoon)*

Summary checklist

I can

- ☐ talk about what helps me to learn.
- ☐ listen to and understand a discussion about role models and give my own views.
- ☐ compare two news reports of the same event.
- ☐ write an email to a friend asking for help with a school project.
- ☐ interpret and give a written account of what is happening in a photo.
- ☐ give a presentation on teenage life.

2 Well-being

In this unit you will…

- **listen to** and **discuss** opinions about food and health
- **read** about the importance of diet and exercise
- **read** and **summarise** a newspaper article about digital devices and sleep
- **talk** about moods and feelings
- **read** and **understand** an article about emotion and behaviour
- **listen to** and **express** opinions about happiness
- **write** a description of a photo
- **give** a presentation about well-being
- **complete** the summary of a story
- **write** your own version of the end of a story.

Getting started

“Well-being means being comfortable, healthy and happy. What do you need to be comfortable, healthy and happy?”

Watch this!

2.1 Food for health

In this lesson you will...

- learn and use vocabulary for talking about food and health
- listen to and discuss opinions about food and health.

- **What do you need to eat to have a balanced diet?**

Reading

1 **How healthy is your diet? Do you agree with these sentences? If not, make them true for you.**

a I think I eat enough protein, but I need to eat more salads and vegetables.
b I eat plenty of fruit.
c I should drink more water and fewer sugary drinks.
d I think I eat too many sweet things. I should probably eat fewer cakes and biscuits.
e I don't want to eat less ice cream, but perhaps I eat too much chocolate!

Language tip

Less is the comparative form of *little*. *Fewer* is the comparative form of *few*. We use *less* with uncountable nouns. We use *fewer* with plural nouns.

*I don't mind eating **less** meat, but I don't want to give it up completely.*

*I should eat **fewer** snacks like crisps and sweets.*

Listening

08

2 **Listen to a podcast about food and health. Why is a balanced diet important?**

3 **Complete the summary of the podcast with the words from the vocabulary box. Then listen again to check. Four of the words are not needed.**

consume	fast food	junk food	nutrition	poverty	undernourished
calories	illness	malnutrition	obesity	food waste	vegetarian

a In some parts of the world, people suffer from .... because they don't have enough to eat.
b Many children are .... and don't get enough protein, vitamins and minerals to grow properly.
c .... is caused by eating more food than your body needs, or eating too much of the wrong kind of food.
d Fast food, processed food and sugary drinks and snacks contain a lot of carbohydrates and fat so they have a lot of ....

e But this kind of food is not the good quality, useful food that your body needs, and that's why it's sometimes called ....

f What's more, this kind of food is quite cheap, so there is a link between obesity and ....

g Eating a .... diet can be just as healthy as a diet that includes meat.

h Reducing .... is important because around one-third of food produced is thrown away.

Speaking

4 **Work in pairs. Discuss these questions.**

a What does Professor Brown advise people to avoid eating, or eat less of, and why?

b What does she advise eating for good nutrition?

c Why does the presenter say 'the world is out of balance'?

5 **Work in pairs. Choose one of the photos and explain to your partner how it relates to what you heard in the podcast.**

Use of English
Abstract nouns

Words like *illness*, *malnutrition* and *poverty* are **abstract nouns**. We usually use abstract nouns without *the* or *a*.

Professor Sheila Brown is an expert in the field of ***health*** *and* ***nutrition****.*

But when you make an abstract noun specific rather than general, you need *the*.

When we think about food for the world and ***the health of the planet****, eating less meat overall is a good option.*

6 **Add *the* where it is needed before the abstract nouns in these sentences.**

a **Malnutrition** affects **health** of children and adults.

b Not having enough to eat leads to **illness** and **disease**.

c Eating too much of the wrong kind of food can also lead to **ill-health**.

d There is a link between **poverty**, **obesity** and **malnutrition**.

e Junk food doesn't provide good **nutrition**.

f We can reduce some of **waste** created by shoppers who are encouraged to buy more than they need.

g People are being made aware of the importance of reducing **waste** worldwide.

7 **Work in groups. Discuss this question: Why is food a personal issue and also a global issue? Try to use the words in the vocabulary box in Exercise 3 in your discussion.**

2.2 Food for thought

In this lesson you will...

- read about the importance of diet and exercise
- use comparative adverbs and scientific vocabulary.

Key words: Science and medicine

bacteria
cells
diabetes
disease
immune system
infection
recovery
viruses

- **What helps you to be healthy?**

Speaking

1 **Work in pairs. Discuss the questions. Then share your ideas with the class.**

a Do you think there's a link between eating regular meals and being able to concentrate in class?

b Why do some people get impatient or bad-tempered when they're hungry?

c The more exercise you do, the better you feel. Do you think this is true?

Reading

2 **Read the extracts from a magazine article. Think of a title for each extract.**

1 According to Dr Brian Stollery of Bristol University, 'Skipping meals leads to low blood sugar, which affects our mood and our ability to think clearly. Our brains use about 20% of the energy used by our bodies. ... We need to keep up a steady supply of energy so that the brain can do its job.'

It is particularly important to eat a good carbohydrate-based breakfast to restore blood sugar levels after a night's sleep. You also need to eat regular meals during the day, because if you don't, the level of serotonin in your body drops. Serotonin is the chemical that helps to keep your moods and emotions in balance.

There is another consequence of skipping meals: you're likely to eat more calories. If you don't eat regularly, your blood sugar levels drop, so you crave sweet, carbohydrate-rich snacks, full of calories. Eating a lot of these snacks can lead to serious health problems such as diabetes or heart disease.

2 Studies have found that people who do sport in their free time appear to be healthier and catch coughs and colds less frequently than people who are less active. Moderate exercise helps the immune cells to circulate around the body more quickly and therefore helps to kill bacteria and viruses more efficiently. However, there is also evidence that too much exercise can have the opposite effect. It can suppress the immune system, especially after extreme exercise, making the body more susceptible to illness and less able to fight off disease.

A further point to remember is that if you are ill, you should not exercise too much because your body is already working hard to fight the infection. Putting stress on your system will mean that your recovery is likely to be slower.

3 Match the words with their definitions.

skipping
restore
crave
suppress
susceptible

a likely to be affected by something
b not doing something that you usually do or should do
c stop something working properly
d return something to a good condition
e want something very much

4 Look at the science and medicine key words. They all appear in Exercise 2. Can you work out their meaning from the context? Check in a dictionary if you need to. Are any of the words similar in your language?

Use of English Comparative adjectives and adverbs

Remember that to make **comparative adjectives**, add *-(e)r* to the adjective or use *more* in front of the adjective.

*Your recovery is likely to be slow**er**.*

To make **negative comparisons**, use *less* in front of the adjective.

*Too much exercise makes the body more susceptible to illness and **less able** to fight off disease.*

To make **comparative adverbs**, use *more* and add *-ly* to the adjective.

*Moderate exercise helps the immune cells to circulate around the body **more** quick**ly**.*

To make **negative comparisons**, use *less* in front of the adverb.

*Active people catch coughs and colds **less frequently**.*

5 Make comparative adjectives or adverbs from the words in the box to complete the sentences. Use each word once only.

tired	clear	slow	efficient	likely	strong

a Potatoes, rice and pasta release energy into the body much ***more slowly*** than sweet snacks.
b I wear contact lenses when I play volleyball because I can see .... with them.
c People who do regular exercise have a .... immune system.
d I've started going to bed earlier and I've noticed I'm much .... at school the next day.
e You're .... to have mood swings if you're hungry.
f Students who come to school without having had breakfast work .... during the morning.

Speaking

6 Look again at the questions in Exercise 1. Continue your discussion using the information in the article.

2.3 Are you getting enough sleep?

In this lesson you will...

- read and summarise a newspaper article about digital devices and sleep
- listen to and discuss opinions about sleep.

- **Do you ever find it difficult to get to sleep? Do you ever wake up feeling as if you haven't had enough sleep? Why do you think this is?**

Reading

1 **Read the newspaper article. When can technology be bad for your health?**

Do you text late into the night and reach for your phone as soon as you wake up?

Many adults now spend more hours of the day using laptops and phones than they do asleep, a survey has revealed.

People spend an average of 8 hours 21 minutes sleeping a day – but spend an average of 8 hours 41 minutes on media devices.

The majority (81%) of phone users have their phones switched on all the time, even in bed, they said.

And four in ten adults and teenagers said there had been occasions when they checked their phone in the night after it woke them up.

They also spend more time each morning checking emails and using the internet than eating breakfast or taking care of their appearance.

Experts have warned that this means that people are not getting enough quality sleep, which has a direct effect on their health.

They have warned that over time, a continued lack of sleep can lead to a weakened immune system and an increased risk of heart disease, high blood pressure and diabetes.

It can also make a person more susceptible to mental health problems such as anxiety and depression.

Dr Nerina Ramlakhan, a sleep and energy coach, advises turning off all technological devices at least 60–90 minutes before going to sleep in order to give the mind time to wind down.

And it's not just adults who are at risk. In a recent focus group of almost 500 students aged 13–15, held by Dr Ramlakhan, an alarming number complained of sleep problems and feeling exhausted.

Of those who complained, almost 80 per cent were using phones and other technology in bed.

She advises keeping the bedroom tech-free to avoid future health issues.

She said: 'Your bedroom is one of the most important factors when it comes to getting a great night's sleep. Banishing technology from the bedroom is one of the easiest things people can do to promote a relaxing sleep environment and ensure they're getting enough rest for the body to recover overnight.'

2 **Work in pairs. Find the words and phrases in the article. Work out their meaning from the context.**

a taking care of their appearance
b wind down
c at risk
d focus group
e exhausted
f banishing
g promote

3 **Answer these questions.**

a How docs the average amount of time people spend using digital devices each day compare with how long they sleep each night?
b How many of the people who were questioned for the survey said they never switched their phone off?
c How many people said that they checked their phone during the night?
d How can using digital devices affect eating habits?
e What are the dangers of letting technology interrupt your sleep?
f What should you do to prepare for a good night's sleep?
g What problems did the students in the focus group have?
h What should you avoid having in the bedroom, according to the article?

Writing

4 **Write a summary of the newspaper article. Use the questions in Exercise 3 to help you.**

Speaking

09

5 **Work in groups. Use the questions below to discuss the article and your views about sleep. To help you, you can listen to two students discussing the newspaper article with their teacher.**

a What do you think of this article?
b Do you wake up during the night to check your phone?
c Do you feel that you get enough sleep? Do you ever feel tired during the day because you haven't had enough sleep?
d What do you think is the best way of avoiding stress and anxiety?
e What else helps you to get a good night's sleep?
f Is having a midday nap (a short sleep) a good idea? Why?

2.4 Moods and feelings

In this lesson you will...

- use words and phrases to talk about moods and feelings
- speculate about how people are feeling and why, using *might have, must have*, etc.

a

b

c

d

e

f

- **How do you feel today? What kind of things influence the way you feel?**

Vocabulary

1 **How do you think the people in the photos are feeling? Write an adjective for each photo. Compare your ideas. Did you all write the same words?**

2 **Work with a partner. Put the words and phrases that have a similar meaning into groups. Make a separate list of those that don't fit into a group.**

angry
annoyed
anxious
apprehensive
bored
confused
delighted
depressed
disappointed
ecstatic
excited
embarrassed
a bit down
frightened
furious
in a bad mood
miserable
mixed up
nervous
sad
terrified
thrilled
upset
worried

3 **Compare the words and phrases in your list with what your classmates have written. Explain and justify your choices.**

Pair 1: ***We've put*** **angry, annoyed, furious** ***and*** **in a bad mood** ***in the same group.***

Pair 2: ***We didn't include*** **in a bad mood** ***because that's different from being*** **angry, annoyed** ***or*** **furious.**

4 **Are there any more words or phrases you can use now to describe the people in the photos in Exercise 1?**

5 **Find a photo in Exercise 1 to match each of these descriptions.**

a She's absolutely furious. Something bad must have happened. She might have just finished some work on her laptop and it's crashed so she's lost all her work.

b He looks a bit down. I think he's had some news and it can't have been good news.

Use of English ***must have, might have, can't have*** **+ past participle**

You can use:

- ***must have*** to talk about things you feel sure have happened. *Something bad* ***must have*** *happened.*
- ***might have*** to talk about things that have perhaps happened. *She* ***might have*** *won a competition.*
- ***can't have*** to talk about things you feel sure haven't happened. *It* ***can't have*** *been good news.*

6 **Use *must have, might have* and *can't have* to write a sentence about each person in the photos in Exercise 1.**

Reading

7 **Read the following paragraph. Which of the following would be a good title for it?**

- Why people get depressed
- Language and emotions
- Positive thinking

People of all ages and from different cultures have far more words to express negative emotions, such as sadness, than they have to express positive emotions, such as happiness. When Professor Robert Schrauf of Penn State University asked people to make a list of adjectives expressing emotions, they wrote down words such as *happy, sad, angry, excited, afraid, anxious, surprised, depressed, grumpy, optimistic* and *satisfied*. The list showed that about half of all the words that people use to express emotions are negative, 30 per cent are positive and 20 per cent are neutral.

Speaking and listening

10

8 **Work in groups. Discuss the following question: Why do you think languages have more words for negative emotions than positive emotions? Then listen to the podcast. Did you come up with similar ideas?**

Writing

9 **Summarise the point of view expressed in the podcast.**

The reason that you hear more words for negative emotions than positive emotions is that …

2.5 Keep a cool head

In this lesson you will...

- read and understand an article about emotion and behaviour
- use intensifiers and strong adjectives.

- **What do you think of as good behaviour? What do you consider to be bad behaviour?**

Reading

1 **Read the article. What interests the journalist about the Inuit people?**

CALM ADULTS, CALM CHILDREN

The Inuit people, who live in the Arctic regions of Greenland, Canada and Alaska, are good role models for keeping a cool head. For the Inuit, to show annoyance is considered bad behaviour; to get angry and shout is totally unacceptable.

A science journalist, Michaeleen Doucleff, who visited the Arctic because she'd read about the way Inuit people bring up their children, noticed a sense of calm generally throughout the community. She said that Inuit parents never shout at small children. Instead, they use stories and role play to help the children learn how to deal with emotions. Children develop patience and empathy by working out how to resolve disagreements; they learn how to manage anger and get on with other people.

Teaching children self-control is particularly valued in communities where interdependence and collaboration are considered important.

By contrast, in societies where competitiveness is seen as necessary for achieving success, expressing emotions is less likely to be discouraged.

Professor Frances Jenson, an expert in the field of neurology, says that while children and teenagers are growing up, their brains are building connections to allow for increasingly complex processes. This makes them highly susceptible to feeling strong emotions. She advises that parents should keep calm and not react to emotional outbursts from their teenage children with an equally emotional response.

16 **empathy:** the ability to imagine how other people feel

21 **interdependence:** helping each other

22 **collaboration:** working together

26 **competitiveness:** wanting to be better than other people

31 **neurology:** the study of the body's nervous system and how the brain works

35 **susceptible to:** likely to be affected by

2 **Answer each question about the text using one word or phrase.**

- a In which area of the world do the Inuit people live?
- b Which emotion should not be shown in their community?
- c What do Inuit parents not do when bringing up their children?
- d What aspect of other cultures does the article contrast with interdependence and collaboration in Inuit communities?
- e How do children and teenagers sometimes react while their brains are developing and building connections?

Speaking

3 **Work in pairs. Use these questions to discuss the article.**

- a Why do you think the journalist wrote the article?
- b What positive results of Inuit parenting are mentioned?
- c How does the article compare parenting in the Inuit communities with that of other places?
- d Why do you think the writer included the last paragraph?

4 **Work in pairs. Ask and answer the questions.**

- a What kind of things do you find particularly irritating?
- b What kind of behaviour do you consider to be totally unacceptable?
- c Can you think of anything that's happened recently that you found really annoying?
- d What makes you very angry? Is there anything that makes you feel absolutely furious?
- e Do you think it's possible to be extremely empathetic and also highly competitive?

5 **Work in groups. Discuss these questions.**

- a How do you think parents should deal with their children's bad behaviour?
- b What is empathy? How important do you think it is in families, in friendships and in the wider community?
- c Do you think children need to learn self-control? Why?
- d Should children be encouraged to be competitive or not? Why?

Key words: Psychology

noun
anger
annoyance
bad behaviour
competitiveness
empathy
self-control

adjective
angry
annoyed, annoying
badly behaved
competitive
empathetic
self-controlled

Use of English
Strong adjectives and intensifiers

Strong adjectives are words like *fascinating* (very interesting), *excellent* (very good) and *terrible* (very bad).

What do these strong adjectives mean?

delicious ***very tasty***
delighted, thrilled
furious
hilarious
huge, gigantic, enormous
starving
tiny, minute

Intensifiers

We don't use *very* before strong adjectives to intensify them. We use words like *absolutely, completely, extremely, particularly, really* and *totally.*

*To get angry and shout is **totally** unacceptable.*

2.6 How to be happy

In this lesson you will...

- listen to and express opinions about happiness.

- **What makes you feel happy?**

Listening

11

1 **Listen to four people talking about happiness. Choose one thing they say that is true for you.**

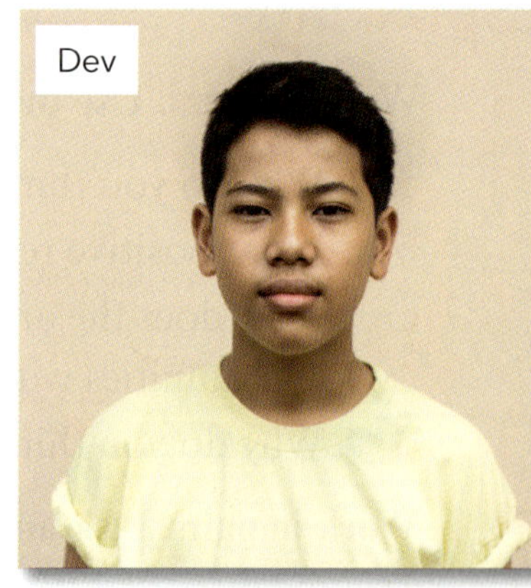

2 **Listen again. What does each person talk about?**

a supportive family	getting involved in activities with others
bad behaviour	physical and mental well-being
bullying	stress and anxiety
friendship	talking in front of other people

3 **Who gives each of these opinions?**

a I don't think you can expect to feel really happy all the time. Sometimes you just feel OK, and that's fine.

b Friends make you laugh when you feel a bit down. They support you when you're worried or when you don't feel confident.

c I feel uncomfortable with situations when people get angry or behave badly and disrupt lessons at school.

d It's fun to be with other people and do things you enjoy.

e I find that just sharing the problem with a friend helps me feel much happier.

f I think being happy is a combination of lots of things: feeling well physically and also mentally, so that you feel you can do your best and enjoy life.

Speaking

4 **Work in pairs. Take turns to ask and answer these questions.**

a What makes you feel really happy?
b What makes you feel unhappy, uncomfortable, worried, depressed or just a bit down?
c How do you deal with difficult situations and things that make you feel unhappy?
d Overall, what would you say is the most important aspect of being happy?

Writing

5 **Write your own opinions on how to be happy to email to the podcast presenter. Use your answers to the questions in Exercise 4 to help you.**

New Message

From:

To: Adrienne Hunter Cc Bcc

Dear Mrs Hunter

I'm writing in response to your podcast on how to be happy. I feel really happy when I …

I think … also helps you to be happy because …

I sometimes feel a bit … when … but to deal with situations like that, I just …

Overall, I would say that the most important aspect is …

Best wishes

…

Send

Speaking and writing tip

We use the verb *get* a lot, particularly in informal speaking and writing. Here are some examples from the podcast you listened to.

*I've **got** a really supportive family.*

*They encourage me to **get involved in** activities like sports and drama.*

*I can **get** quite anxious sometimes.*

*I like being at home, just **getting on with** things I'm interested in.*

*I feel uncomfortable with situations when people **get** angry or behave badly.*

*I **get on with** most people.*

Use *really* to add emphasis.

*I'm lucky because I've got a **really** supportive family.*

Use *quite* and *a bit* to qualify ideas.

*I'm **quite** sociable.*

*I get **a bit** nervous about things like talking in front of other people.*

2.7 Improve your writing

In this lesson you will…

- write about a photo.

1 **Work in pairs. Discuss what is happening in this photo and the reasons for it.**

2 **Read the description of this photo on the opposite page.**

3 **Write a paragraph about each of the photos on the opposite page using the questions below.**

- Who is in the photo?
- Where is he / she?
- What is he / she doing?
- What might / could / must have happened (before the photo was taken)?
- What might happen next?

Remember that there are no right or wrong answers. You can use your imagination and give your own ideas about the details in the photo.

4 **Ask your partner to read your description. Read your partner's description and check that it answers all the questions in Exercise 3.**

5 **Add suggestions and corrections. Then write a final draft.**

Write a title for your description.

Say who is in the photo and what is happening.

Speculate to explain what might have happened before the photo was taken.

Add detail to your description by giving information and your own ideas about the situation.

Speculate about what might happen next.

A midday nap!

The boy in the photo has fallen asleep during a lesson at school.

He must have gone to bed late and he might have woken up during the night to check his phone, so he didn't get enough sleep.

He might not have had time to eat breakfast. If you don't have breakfast, you feel tired during the day and your brain doesn't work as well as it should do, so you can't concentrate.

Perhaps the student sitting next to him will wake him up before the teacher notices!

2.8 Project challenge

Project 1: A good night's sleep

You are going to make a poster giving advice about sleep for teenagers.

1 Work in pairs.

2 Discuss these questions.
- Why is it important to get a good night's sleep?
- What happens if you don't get enough sleep or if your sleep is interrupted?
- What helps you to sleep well?
- What should you avoid doing if you want to sleep well?

3 Use your answers to the questions to write a draft of 4–6 points giving advice.

4 Look back at Lesson 2.3. Can you add more information to your text? Can you improve what you have written by using vocabulary from the lesson?

5 Find photos or drawings to illustrate your advice.

6 Write a final version.
- Have you spelled words correctly?
- Is the grammar correct?
- Is the punctuation correct?

- Was it helpful to answer the questions in Step 2 of the instructions? Why?
- How did working in pairs help you with this project?

Project 2: What makes you happy?

You are going to give a presentation about happiness and well-being.

1 Work in groups. Read the information about a study of what makes teenagers happy. Write notes on the key information.

> What makes teenagers happy, according to research, are the simple things in life.
>
> A study conducted for the World Health Organization found that a healthy lifestyle increases teenage happiness. The study surveyed more than 200,000 young people and found that 80% of them reported feeling positive about their lives and experienced high satisfaction levels. It linked healthy eating and physical activity with feeling happy. The study showed that higher consumption of fruit and vegetables and lower consumption of chips, sweets and soft drinks were associated with greater happiness. The more hours of sports that young people participated in per week, the happier they were.

2 What else makes teenagers happy? Look back at what you have read in this unit and note down key points. Use the internet or other sources to find more information.

3 Organise your information in short sections.

4 Use quotations and information as evidence to explain and back up your opinions. For example: ***'According to a study by the World Health Organization, a healthy diet and taking part in sports make teenagers happier.'***

5 You could also do a survey among your friends or students in another class to find out what makes them happy. Record their answers to include in your presentation. ***We asked 20 students in our school: 'What makes you feel positive about your life?' Of those questioned, 75% said that … made them feel ….***

6 Decide who will present each section.

7 Rehearse your presentation as a group. Suggest any improvements.

8 Give your presentation to the class. Then ask for questions and feedback.

- How did the work you had done in the unit help you to write your presentation?

2.9 Fiction

'A Rainbow in Silk' is a traditional story from Uzbekistan.

Reading

1 **Read and listen to the first part of the story on the opposite page. What does each part of the illustration show?**

Vocabulary

2 **Look back at the words and phrases to describe feelings in Lesson 2.4. Answer these questions.**

a Which **adjectives** are used in the story to describe the Beg's counsellor? Which **adverbs** are used to show the way he reacted to the Beg's demand?

b Which other words and phrases from Lesson 2.4 could you use to describe the Beg and his counsellor?

3 **Complete this summary of the story so far. Try to include some of the words in the glossary.**

The Beg had everything he could have wanted. He had plenty of money, beautiful buildings, enough food for his people and no enemies, but …

So he … The counsellor summoned …

However, …

Finally, …

The poor counsellor …

However, …

Speaking and writing

4 **Work in groups.**

a Discuss this question: What do you think the counsellor's idea was?

b Write your version of the end of the story.

[4] orchard: a piece of land where fruit trees are grown
[6] gleam: to shine softly
[6] turquoise: greenish-blue
[8] foreign: from another country
[8] enemy: a person or a country you are fighting
[10] stand: to accept, tolerate
[14] spoilt child: a child who always gets what they want
[16] horrified: very shocked
[20] hiss: to make a long noise like the letter 's'
[21] counsellor: a person who gives advice, help and support
[23] summon: to order someone to come
[25] tumblers: people who entertain by doing somersaults etc.
[26] star-gazers: an old-fashioned word for 'astronomers'
[27] potion: a drink that has a special effect on someone
[32] scribble: to write very quickly
[32] furiously: (here) at great speed
[34] yawn: to take a deep breath with your mouth wide open
[40] gasp: to make a noise by suddenly breathing in
[41] snatch: to take something away from someone quickly
[41] smash: to break into pieces
[44] weaver: someone who makes cloth or carpets
[53] wear on: to pass very slowly (used to describe time)
[62] kneel: to go down on your knees (*past tense:* knelt)
[67] graciously: politely
[68] dismiss: to tell someone they are allowed to go

A Rainbow in Silk

There was once a Beg – an important ruler – who had everything that any man could have wanted. He rode about the city on a magnificent white horse and admired its orchards and gardens, and the fine mosques whose domes gleamed blue and turquoise in the morning sun. The treasuries were full, the harvests were good, the Beg had no foreign enemies to worry about. But the Beg was very, very bored.

One day he could stand it no longer. He sent for his counsellor, a man who had served him well for many years.

'I want something new!' he said, and tears came to his eyes like a spoilt child. 'I'm bored! There's nothing to do any more!'

His counsellor was horrified. He had never had to deal with a situation like this before. He scratched his chin anxiously. 'Well,' he said miserably, 'I really don't know, Your Highness.'

'Then think of something!' the Beg hissed, and turned away. The counsellor bowed, then retreated thankfully. What had got into his master? Straight away he summoned all the best artists and craftsmen in the town, all the writers and poets, all the tumblers and clowns, all the star-gazers and doctors, and asked their advice.

The doctors gave him potions which they said were recipes for Eternal Life.

'Hah! Eternal Life! Well, I shan't know, shall I? Not till you're dead and gone!' And he gave the doctors such a nasty look that they hurried away.

The writers and poets scribbled furiously and begged to be allowed to read their new works to the Beg. But he yawned loudly whenever they tried.

Everybody was losing patience with the Beg, but of course they didn't dare show it.

The glass-blower brought a swan which he had made of fine blue glass. Everyone in the court gasped as he carried it in, it was so beautiful. The Beg reached out to snatch it and smash it, but the glass-blower managed to keep it just out of his reach.

The carpet weavers worked day and night in teams to complete a fine and huge carpet showing the Beg on his favourite horse. But the Beg wasn't interested.

Finally, he summoned his adviser again. 'You've got one more day!' he roared at him. 'Don't you understand? I'M BORED! I want something new! By tomorrow! Or else!'

The counsellor was terrified.

The night wore on, and the poor counsellor didn't sleep at all.

At last the first rays of the morning sun crept through his window. The counsellor's eyes were wet with tears. And as the light touched the teardrops on his eyelashes, suddenly a brilliant rainbow appeared before his eyes.

'That's it!' He sat up in bed, excited beyond belief.

He ran into the Beg's presence and knelt down before him. 'Your Highness, I think I can do it! I have a wonderful idea! Just give me a few more days.'

Even the Beg could see that the counsellor was excited. The Beg nodded graciously and dismissed him.

Listen

13

6 **Listen to how the original story ends and answer these questions.**

a The counsellor had an idea for something that would make the Beg happy. Where did he get the idea from?

b The Beg says, 'This is what I've been waiting for!' Why do you think the counsellor's gift is a success?

Audio words

dyer: someone who uses dye (a substance that changes the colour of cloth, hair, etc.)

tailor: someone who makes clothes

eagerly: in a way that shows you want something very much

robe: a long, loose piece of clothing

shimmer: to shine with a soft light that makes an object look as if it is shaking a little

a sigh of relief: a noise you make when you breathe out, showing that you are no longer worried about something

triumphantly: showing that you are very excited about a success or a victory

joyfully: with joy, great happiness

twirl: to move in circles

throne: the chair that a ruler sits on

dignified: calm and serious

Language tip

You can use *so* with an adjective and *such* with a noun phrase to give them emphasis.

*The glass swan was **so beautiful**.*

*I am in **such a good mood** today!*

You can make them even stronger by adding a clause with *that*:

*The counsellor was **so pleased** and **excited that** he wasn't afraid of the Beg now.*

*The Beg gave the doctors **such a nasty look that** they hurried away.*

Writing

7 **Read your version of the end of the story again. Is there anything you would like to change? If the answer is 'Yes', go to question a. If the answer is 'No', go to question b.**

a What do you want to change, and why? Rewrite your revised version. Can you include a sentence with *so* or *such*?

b What do you remember about how the original story ended? Use the glossary to help you to write it.

Check your progress

General knowledge quiz

1 On average, how many hours a day do adults spend on media devices?

a under seven b over eight c over ten

2 What is 'the immune system'?

3 Why is this kind of food called 'junk food'?

4 How much of the food produced in the world is wasted?

a a tenth b a third c a quarter

5 How much of your body's energy is used by your brain?

a 10% b 20% c 30%

6 What is serotonin?

7 Do languages generally have more adjectives for positive emotions or negative emotions?

8 Where do the Inuit people live?

9 What is considered bad behaviour in the Inuit community?

10 What do you call the study of the body's nervous system and how the brain works?

Vocabulary

Moods and feelings

1 **Complete each sentence with the correct adjective.**

bored	thrilled	confused
furious	depressed	apprehensive

a I was really angry. In fact, I was absolutely ....

b He was feeling a bit down, but he wasn't ....

c Rania's mum was delighted that Rania had passed her final music exam. 'I'm absolutely ....,' she said.

d I wasn't really worried about starting at a new school. I was just a bit ....

e When you become a teenager you can feel mixed up at times and even quite ....

f I'm not in a bad mood. I'm just .... because I've got nothing to do.

Health and illness

2 **Match the medical words to their definitions.**

bacteria	a	a disease in part of your body that is caused by bacteria or a virus
cell	b	protected against a disease
diabetes	c	the smallest living part of an animal or a plant
immune	d	very small living things that sometimes cause disease
infection	e	when you feel better again after an illness
recovery	f	an illness in which the body cannot control the level of sugar in the blood

Use of English

1 Choose the correct option.

a You catch coughs and colds ***less frequently / less frequent*** if you're an active person.

b If you don't stay in bed when you've got flu, your recovery is likely to be ***slower / more slowly***.

c If you do regular exercise, your heart works ***more efficient / more efficiently***.

d Exercise helps the immune cells to circulate round the body ***more effective / more effectively.***

e If you were ***more active / more actively***, I'm sure you'd feel better.

2 Chose the correct option.

a It ***must have / can't have*** been easy to learn a new language in three months.

b She ***must have / might have*** won the race if she hadn't fallen over in the last 50 metres.

c They ***might have / can't have*** got lost. I gave them very clear directions.

d The violinist played the piece perfectly. She ***can't have / must have*** practised a lot before the concert.

3 Replace the underlined words with the word in brackets and a suitable adjective from the box.

annoyed	exhausted	furious
successful	terrified	

a Lisa always goes by train because she is very frightened of flying. (*really*)

b By the time we'd finished the 30 kilometre walk, we were very tired. (*completely*)

c My dad was very angry when his car was stolen from outside our house. (*absolutely*)

d We were very unhappy that there were no vegetarian options because our friends don't eat meat. (*particularly*)

e My sister is a very good swimmer; she's won lots of championships. (*highly*)

Summary checklist

I can

- ☐ explain the importance of food and exercise for health.
- ☐ summarise a newspaper article.
- ☐ discuss emotions and feelings.
- ☐ give advice about sleep.
- ☐ prepare and give an evidence-based presentation.
- ☐ complete a story.

3 Tourism

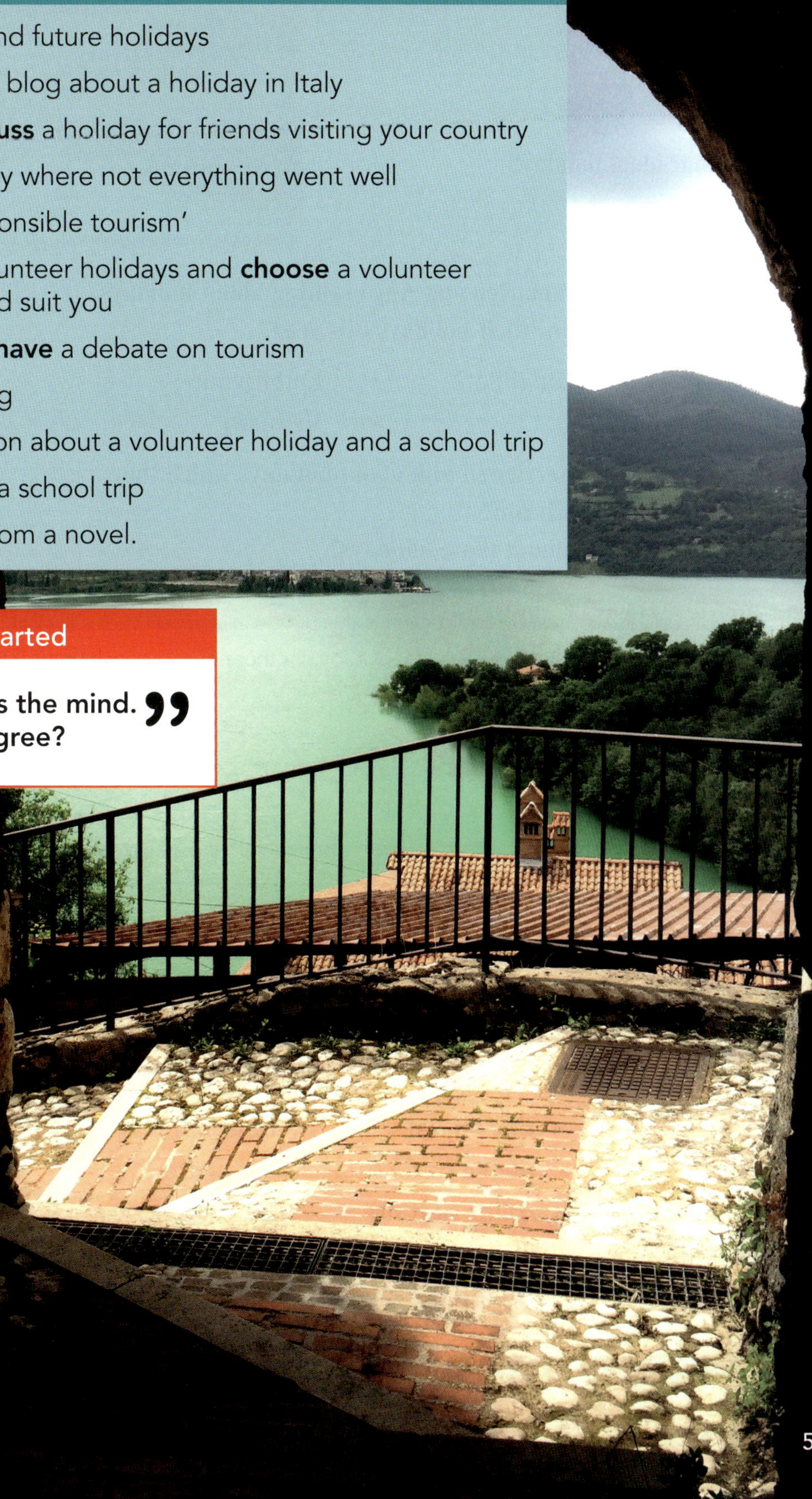

In this unit you will...

- **talk** about past and future holidays
- **read** a teenager's blog about a holiday in Italy
- **think of** and **discuss** a holiday for friends visiting your country
- **describe** a holiday where not everything went well
- **learn** about 'responsible tourism'
- **compare** two volunteer holidays and **choose** a volunteer holiday that would suit you
- **prepare for** and **have** a debate on tourism
- **write** a travel blog
- **give** a presentation about a volunteer holiday and a school trip
- **write** a report of a school trip
- **read** an extract from a novel.

Getting started

"Travel broadens the mind." Do you agree?

Watch this!

3.1 On holiday

In this lesson you will...

- talk about past and future holidays
- use compound nouns and multi-word verbs to describe a holiday.

- **What is your ideal holiday?**

Listening

14 **1** **Listen to Bruno, Mariam, Ren and Anya talking about holidays. Where are they going for their holidays this year?**

- Mount Fuji National Park
- Dubrovnik
- Jeddah
- Vietnam

2 **Two of the students interviewed talk about holidays which they went on last year. Which two? And what do they say about those holidays?**

Language tip

When you're listening, it's important to be able to distinguish past events from present and future events.

Remember Compound nouns

A **compound noun** is usually a noun followed by another noun: *a beach umbrella, a car park*. Other types of compound noun include:

- adjective + noun — *hot springs*
- verb ending in *-ing* + noun — *a swimming pool*
- noun + verb ending in *-ing* — *ice skating*

Compound nouns can also be formed from multi-word verbs: *a passer-by, a runner-up*.

Vocabulary

14 **3** **Listen again. For each person, choose the one thing that they do <u>not</u> mention.**

Bruno	Mariam	Ren	Anya
eco hotel	day trip(s)	national park	swimming pool
water sports	picnic basket	campsite	beach umbrella
windsurfing	roller skating	hot springs	sightseeing tour
waterskiing	ice skating	insect repellent	boat trip(s)
first-aid kit	theme park	tennis courts	

4 Answer these questions.

a What can you tell about the people interviewed from what they say about their holidays?

b Who are you most like: Bruno, Mariam, Ren or Anya?

Remember Multi-word verbs (phrasal and prepositional verbs)

Multi-word verbs are used a lot in English. They help to make your conversation sound more natural. The students interviewed in Exercise 1 used quite a few multi-word verbs.

5 Can you remember who said each of the following?

a 'You can **look round** the shops.'

b 'I could have **stayed on**!'

c 'I don't mind **going back** to the same place.'

d 'My cousins live there, so I can **catch up with** them.'

e 'We'll **eat out** every night.'

f 'They find it very hard **to take time off** work.'

g '**I'm looking forward to** hearing all their news.'

h 'I **ended up** going to the doctor!'

6 Work with a partner. Can you replace the words in bold in Exercise 5 to show their meaning? You can make other changes if necessary.

You can go from shop to shop, looking at what they've got.

Speaking

7 Work in groups. Talk about holidays. Listen, and take notes on what each other says.

- Say where you are going on holiday, or where you would like to go.
- If you can, refer to a past holiday too.
- Use some of the compound nouns in Exercise 3.
- Try to include some multi-word verbs, like the ones in Exercise 5.
- Try to include some expressions with *go*:
  - go camping, sightseeing, swimming, climbing
  - go on a boat trip, a day trip, a tour
- At the end of your conversation, summarise what each other said, and check that it is correct.

3.2 A holiday to remember

In this lesson you will...

- read a teenager's blog about a holiday in Italy
- think of and discuss a holiday for friends visiting your country.

Key words: European art and architecture

amphitheatre
arch (*plural:* arches)
fresco (*plural:* frescoes)
the medieval period (about 500–1400 CE)
the Renaissance (about 1400–1600 CE)

- **Apart from relaxing and enjoying yourself, what else can you do on holiday?**

Reading

1 **Read Elena's blog. Where was she when she took the photo at the bottom of the opposite page? What does it show?**

When my parents told me that we were going on a cycling holiday in Italy, I thought, 'Oh no! Cycling!' Even worse, it was a trip called 'The art and architecture of northern Italy'. How boring!

Day 1
We arrived in Mantua. It's surrounded by three lakes. In the centre, there are four main squares and two huge palaces. Some of the buildings date from medieval times. We went to the Palazzo Ducale, where the ruling Gonzaga family lived for just under 400 years. It was once the largest palace in Europe, with over a thousand people living there! There was one room with frescoes that were just amazing. They were painted in 1474 by a Renaissance artist called Andrea Mantegna. One fresco shows the Gonzaga family. There are two arches. In the one on the left, you can see Ludovico and Barbara Gonzaga with their children. Ludovico is holding a letter and talking to a man who may be his brother. The people look so real. And when you look up, you see that Mantegna painted the ceiling to make it look as though it's open to the sky!

Day 2 35 km
I could have stayed on in Mantua for another week, but we had a long bike ride ahead of us! The first thing we did was to pick up our bikes. You could have an e-bike (so of course, I did). And your bags are taken from one place to the next by car. Great! So, first we headed north towards Lake Garda, round the lakes, through a nature reserve and along the river. We saw some beautiful birds and the weather was perfect. We stayed at a small, family-run hotel in a village called Borghetto.

Day 3 25 km
Today we did a circular route from the village. There was a cycle track through a park that had a lake and even a maze. We had fun trying to find our way out of the maze! We saw deer. And we had a picnic!

Day 4 40 km
We cycled north towards Lake Garda, along a path by the river, through orchards and vineyards. We stayed in a town with medieval walls on the southern edge of Lake Garda, where we stopped for lunch before heading east to a village just 20 km from Verona.

Day 5 20 km
We cycled into Verona and got ready to explore.

Day 6
Wow! You need more than a day to do a sightseeing tour of Verona! For a start, there's the amazing arena, a Roman amphitheatre, built in the first century, where 20,000 people watched gladiator contests in Roman times. They now have huge open-air opera performances there. Everybody who has read or seen Shakespeare's *Romeo and Juliet* goes to see 'Juliet's house' (even though Juliet didn't exist). People say that if you stand under the balcony and make a wish about love, it will come true. I didn't. I don't believe in all that romantic stuff. Mum said, 'Do you want to look round the shops this afternoon, as it's our last day?' 'No thanks,' I replied, 'this is much more interesting. I want to explore Verona.'

2 **Find these words in the text and try to work out their meaning from the context.**

a palace b fresco c arch d ceiling e amphitheatre

3 **Read the text again and answer these questions.**

a What is the Italian word for 'palace'?
b What impressed Elena most about Mantua?
c What impressed Elena about the travel arrangements?
d Elena doesn't say where she started from on Day 4, but you can work it out. Where was it?
e What impression do you get of the landscape through which Elena cycled?
f What impression do you get of Elena's character?
g How did the holiday change Elena's mind?

Speaking

4 **Work in groups. Some friends of your family are visiting your country. They want to do a trip like Elena's, walking or cycling, over four, five or six days. In your group, discuss these questions:**

- Where will you recommend them to go?
- How will you recommend them to travel?
- What can they see? Think of art and architecture, and give an idea of the historical background (for example, the Islamic Golden Age, the Ming Dynasty).
- Is there anything special they can do?
- Where can they stay?

5 **Compare the trip you have chosen with the trip other groups have chosen. Give reasons to support your choice.**

We chose … because …

3.3 How was your holiday?

In this lesson you will...

- describe a holiday where not everything went well
- learn to use the past continuous passive.

- **For some people, it's exciting to go to new places and to meet people who speak different languages and have different ways of life. For others, it's quite scary. What's your view?**

Listening

15

1 **Listen to Francisco, Li and Sasha talking about their holidays. Did they enjoy their holidays, or did they have mixed feelings?**

2 **Listen again and answer these questions.**

a Why did Francisco's holiday get off to a bad start?

b The plane that Francisco and his family were on didn't get in till 11.30 at night. Why?

c There is an inconsistency in what Francisco says. What is it? (Clue: activities)

d Where did Li go on holiday?

e Li mentions two problems. What were they?

f Which place did Li like best?

g Sasha went to Agadir. Where is Agadir?

h What did Sasha like about Agadir?

i What happened on the way to Paradise Valley, and why wasn't it such a bad experience?

j Who would be the best person to go on holiday with: Francisco, Li or Sasha?

Remember

When someone says one thing and then says something that doesn't match, so that both things can't be true, that is an **inconsistency**.

Use of English Past continuous passive

You already know the past simple active, the past simple passive and the past continuous active.

There is also a **past continuous passive**. (Remember that in Unit 1, you learned the present continuous passive.)

*The car **broke down** (past simple active) in a village while we **were going** (past continuous active) to a place called Paradise Valley.*

*We **were invited** (past simple passive) into the house of one of the people in the village while the car **was being fixed** (past continuous passive).*

3 **Answer these questions, using the past continuous passive.**

a Why did Francisco and his family have to wait three hours for the second plane?

b Why couldn't Li use the swimming pool at the apartment in San Francisco?

c What did the radio announcement tell Li and her family as they were driving to Yosemite?

4 **Look at this list of multi-word verbs used by Francisco, Li and Sasha. Use each one in a sentence about their holidays. Listen again if you need to.**

Francisco
get off (to a bad start)
pick someone up
turn up
take off
turn back
get in

Li
hang out

Sasha
break down
turn out

Speaking

5 **Describe a holiday in which at least one thing went wrong. You can make up the details, and you can make it as humorous as you like!**

- You can use some of the expressions that Francisco, Li and Sasha used.
- Try to include some of the multi-word verbs that they used.
- Try to include at least one verb in the past continuous passive.

Paradise Valley, near Agadir, Morocco

3.4 Responsible tourism

In this lesson you will...

- explain what 'responsible tourism' is, after listening to an interview about it
- use compound adjectives.

- **How can tourism have a bad effect on a place?**

Listening

16

1 **Listen to the interview with Dr Rosa Benavides from the Centre for Responsible Tourism. What is 'responsible tourism'?**

Vocabulary

2 **Look at the words in the list. What is the connection between each of them and responsible tourism?**

a litter
b precious resources
c air conditioning
d accommodation, international hotel chain
e local economy, local produce
f souvenirs
g wildlife products
h endangered species

3 **Listen again and answer these questions.**

a Dr Benavides talks of places that are 'environmentally sensitive'. What sort of places do you think she means?
b She says that tourism 'opens our eyes and our minds'. What do you think she means?
c She gives two examples of 'irresponsible tourism'. What are they?
d According to Dr Benavides, where does a responsible tourist stay and how should they choose what to eat?

e What do the two pictures on the opposite page show, and how do they relate to the topic of the interview?

f What can you say about the attitude of the interviewer? Does he seem to agree or disagree with Dr Benavides, or is he neutral? Would you say he is a sympathetic interviewer?

Use of English Compound adjectives

Compound adjectives are adjectives made up of more than one word:

the ***recently established*** *Centre for Responsible Tourism*

Remember that adjectives, including compound adjectives, can be used after the verb *be* and other 'link' verbs, like *look*, *seem*, *taste* and *feel*:

The sea ***looks pale grey*** *in this light.*

Language tip

The opposite of *dark blue* is *light blue* or *pale blue*.

The opposite of *open-minded* is *narrow-minded*.

4 **These compound adjectives are all used in the interview you have just heard. What does each of them refer to?**

a environmentally sensitive
Dr Benavides mentions places that are environmentally sensitive.

b family-run

c big-name

d homemade

e open-minded

f locally made

g handmade

h dark blue

Speaking

5 **Work in groups. Role-play the following situation.**

Your teacher has asked you to explain responsible tourism to the students in another class.

Divide your group into two sub-groups, A and B.

Sub-group A uses the information in the interview to explain and answer questions about responsible tourism. Sub-group B wants to know about responsible tourism and asks questions about it.

3.5 A different type of family holiday

In this lesson you will...

- compare two volunteer holidays
- choose a volunteer holiday that would suit you.

Key words: Environmental studies

coexistence
conservation
monitor
neglect

- **What do you think a 'volunteer holiday' is?**

Reading

1 **Read about two types of holiday. In which countries are the holidays?**

a

We look after horses that have been mistreated, malnourished or neglected. At present, we have over 40 horses. The accommodation for volunteers is just 7 km from the Indian Ocean in one of the most beautiful areas of South Africa. It is a short walk to the farm where the horses live.

You work with horses five days out of seven. You do not need to be an experienced rider, but you need to be comfortable working with horses. You will help the horses to believe again that people can be kind to them, and that they can trust people. You'll take the horses along the beach and along trails. And in your free time, you can enjoy exploring the area, swimming and watching the dolphins!

b

The aim of the Elephant and Wildlife Conservation project in Sri Lanka is simple: to protect the elephants and wildlife that are found in the national park and local communities.

We research the behaviour of wild elephants and work with local farmers and local communities to help them live together peacefully.

You will be doing important conservation work as a volunteer, recording the numbers of elephants and monitoring them carefully to see if they are healthy or have any injuries. You will help to build and mend fences, and you will talk to villagers to find out what is needed for peaceful coexistence.

2 **Match the words in the environmental studies key words box to their meanings.**

a carefully check the progress of something

b the protection of animals, plants and natural areas

c not look after properly

d living together

3 **Answer these questions.**

a What do the two holidays described in Exercise 1 have in common?

b Where might you find the descriptions? In a reference book about animals? In a biology textbook? Somewhere else? Give reasons for your answer.

c Read this extract from the text about elephants. What is implied, but not directly stated?

We research the behaviour of wild elephants and work with local farmers and local communities to help them live together peacefully. … you will talk to villagers to find out what is needed for peaceful coexistence.

d How does the person who wrote the descriptions persuade you that you might enjoy this type of holiday? Choose phrases from each text to illustrate your answer.

e If you were considering one of these holidays, what other information would you need?

Speaking

4 **Work in groups. Discuss these questions.**

a What are the advantages and disadvantages of each of these holidays?

b Which holiday would you choose, and why?

3.6 Is tourism a good thing?

In this lesson you will…

- prepare for and have a debate on tourism
- identify and use participle adjectives.

- **Why do people ask the question, 'Is tourism a good thing?'?**

Reading

1 Read the notes these students have made in preparation for a class debate on tourism.

FOR

- jobs created
- money for businesses (restaurants, shops)
- money for local people (accommodation)
- money to improve roads, infrastructure of developing economies (water supply, power supply)
- money for conservation projects (animals, national parks)
- money to help local traditions survive (handmade souvenirs)
- opens your mind – other cultures, customs: exciting, rewarding; can be really inspired by what you see

AGAINST

- litter, worrying rise in pollution; big hotels, golf courses, etc. (not places for local people)
- popular places lose identity – more tourists than residents sometimes (e.g. Greek islands, Maldives, Venice)
- big businesses move in, money goes to them
- house prices rise – annoying for local people (can't afford them)
- tourism-based economy: jobs only part-time, for part of year
- most tourists not interested in traditions of other places – places change for the worse (e.g. some coastal resorts in Spain)

Writing

2 The notes in Exercise 1 are in note form. How would you express them in full sentences, as if you were writing them in a report?

jobs created	***Jobs are created.***
money for businesses (restaurants, shops)	***There is more money for businesses, such as restaurants and shops.***

Use of English Participle adjectives

Remember the difference between adjectives ending in *-ing* and adjectives ending in *-ed*:

*an **exciting** holiday*

*I am **excited** about going on holiday.*

Find examples of participle adjectives ending in *-ing* and *-ed* in the notes in Exercise 1.

In Lesson 3.4, we looked at compound adjectives. Some of them contained past participles:

run is the **past participle** of the verb *run*

*a family-**run** hotel*

made is the **past participle** of the verb *make*

*locally **made** souvenirs*

Find a compound adjective containing a past participle in the 'against' list in Exercise 1.

Language tip

In Lesson 2.5, you learned about **intensifiers** (*really, extremely, totally*, etc). You can use intensifiers with participle adjectives.

*The increase in pollution is **extremely worrying**.*

*People are **extremely worried** about the increase in pollution.*

Listening

17 **3 Listen to students having a debate on tourism. Each side ('for' and 'against') has a copy of the list in Exercise 1. Each side forgets one thing on the list. What is it?**

4 In your opinion, who makes the most convincing argument: the students 'for' tourism or the students 'against' tourism?

Speaking

5 You are going to debate the motion 'Tourism is a good thing'.

- Your teacher will divide the class into three groups. Group 1 speaks 'for' the motion. Group 2 speaks 'against' the motion. Group 3 can ask questions before voting on whether they are for or against.
- Groups 1 and 2: you can use the notes in Exercise 1 to help you. You can also add your own notes.
- Give examples of what you mean – this can really help your argument.
- Make sure you summarise what the people in your group have said.

3.7 Improve your writing

In this lesson you will...

- write a travel blog.

In Lesson 3.2, you worked in groups to plan a walking or cycling trip for friends of your family who were visiting your country. These are the questions you discussed:

- Where will you recommend them to go?
- How will you recommend them to travel?
- Is there anything special they can do?
- Where can they stay?
- What can they see? Think of art and architecture, and give an idea of the historical background (for example, the Islamic Golden Age, the Ming Dynasty).

1 **Work in the same groups as in Lesson 3.2. Remind yourselves of the trips you discussed.**

I think we recommended them to go from … to …

Trip: The Lycian Way, South-West Turkey

When I realised that we were going on a walking holiday, I thought, 'Oh no! Walking!' Then I saw the route on the map and it was even worse: 18 kilometres a day! Oh well, at least your bags are taken on from place to place.

Day 1

We arrived in Beycik. It's a lovely village in a national park. Our rooms all had sea views and there was a swimming pool. This was really nice!

Day 2 18 km

Today we headed towards Çirali. It was a long walk, but it was so interesting. We went along a river bank, then across the river and climbed to the top of a hill. Guess what we saw! This!

Yes, flames coming out of the ground at a place called Chimaera! It was as if the earth was on fire. It was amazing! The last part of the walk was through orchards. We arrived at our hotel at about 5 o'clock. It was a beach hotel, so we went straight down to the sea for a swim. Lovely!

2 **You decide to go on the trip with the friends of your family. Plan the trip.**

- From … to …?
- Number of days?
- Walking or cycling?
- Accommodation?

3 **You are now on the trip. Write a blog, like Elena's blog in Lesson 3.2. To help you, look at another example of a blog below. It was written by a Turkish teenager on a walk in south-west Turkey.**

Try to include:

We headed towards	**Prepositions of movement:**	**A mixture of past tenses:**
We saw	*towards, along,*	*we arrived, we were given,*
We stayed at (a hotel) / in (a town)	*through, into,*	*while we were having lunch,*
We stopped for lunch at / in	*round …*	*while the dinner was being prepared, …*

4 **Answer these questions.**

a How many of the suggestions in Exercise 3 have you managed to include?

b Find the exclamation marks (!) in Elena's blog. How many are there and why does she use them? Can you include any in your blog?

Walking from Beycik to the lighthouse at Gelidonya

Day 3
Today we went swimming again and explored the remains of the Roman city of Olympos, including the House of Mosaics. Wow!

Day 4 17 km
We walked from Çirali to Adrasan. On the way, we saw Roman temples. I think I want to learn more about Roman times. In Adrasan, we stayed at a very friendly, family-run hotel.

Day 5
Today we did a circular walk from Adrasan and we went on a boat trip in the afternoon. Very relaxing!

Day 6 18 km
We walked from Adrasan to the Gelidonya Lighthouse. We walked through a forest, where we stopped for a picnic lunch, and along rocky paths before finally reaching the lighthouse, where we were picked up and taken to our hotel. What a great week! I could have stayed on!

3.8 Project challenge

Project 1: A volunteer holiday

You are going to give a presentation about a volunteer holiday.

For this project, you will need to find out about volunteer holidays in your country or in a country you would like to visit.

1 Work in small groups. Choose a country and find out about volunteer holidays for you, your class and a group of teachers from your school.

2 Choose the type of holiday that you would enjoy. For example:

- wildlife conservation
  animals: working with endangered species, working in situations where animals come into conflict with humans, helping with animals that have been injured plants: helping to look after natural areas (nature reserves, national parks), planting trees

- the built environment
  education: helping to repair school buildings, build playgrounds and sports facilities
  culture: helping to restore buildings of historic interest.

3 You only have three minutes to present your choice. You can't use slides or visuals. Decide on the following:

- Are you going to write out the whole text of what you're going to say, or are you just going to write notes?
- Who is going to talk – one person or several people?
- How can you make your talk different?

4 Try to include the following phrases in your presentation:

Have you thought about …?

You will be helping to …

Thanks to your efforts, …

The aim of … is simple:

In your free time, you can enjoy …

- How did not being able to use slides and visuals affect your presentation?

Project 2: A school trip

You are going to give a presentation and write a report about a school trip.

Your class recently went on a school trip. Your teacher has asked you to give a presentation about it to parents at a parents' evening and to write a report.

It can be an account of a real school trip or an imagined one.

1 Work in groups. First, answer these questions.

  a Where did you go?
  b How long did you go for? (minimum: a weekend; maximum: a week)
  c What was the purpose of the trip?
  d Where did you stay? What was the accommodation like?
  e What was good about the trip?
  f What was not so good?
  g What did you learn?
  h Why are school trips important?

The presentation

2 You can use slides and visuals. Plan your presentation. Will you present what you have to say in the same order as the questions in Step 1?

3 Decide who will write the notes for the presentation, who will find the pictures and who will create the slides.

4 Prepare your presentation.

5 Check your notes and your slides to make sure they are correct.

6 Give the presentation.

The report

The report is for your teacher. In addition to the questions in Exercise 1, you are also going to answer this question: 'Would you change anything if the school did the trip again?'

7 Using the notes you made for your presentation, plan your report. Remember to answer the question about whether you would change anything next time.

8 Write a draft of the report. Choose a more formal style for your report. For example, in your presentation you might have described something as 'absolutely amazing' and talked about 'hanging out' with friends. In a written report, you could say something was 'a great success' and that you enjoyed 'being together' with friends.

9 Swap drafts with another group and make corrections and suggestions.

10 Write the final version of your report.

- What is the value of having other people comment on your work?

3.9 Fiction

***The Summer Book* by Tove Jansson**

The writer and artist Tove Jansson was born into a Swedish-speaking family in Finland. She wrote *The Summer Book* in Swedish in 1972. It was first published in English in 1974.

The photo shows her house on the island of Klovharu, in the Gulf of Finland.

Reading and listening

18

1 Read and listen to the beginning of Chapter 1 of *The Summer Book*. The setting is a very small island in the Gulf of Finland. Do Sophia and her grandmother live there, or are they there on holiday? How do you know?

2 Answer these questions.

a Who is 'she' in the first paragraph? (line 08)

b What impression do you get of the grandmother's character?

c What impression do you get of Sophia's character?

d Sophia asks, "Will they dig a hole?" What does she mean?

3 granite: a very hard grey, pink or black rock
3 to steam: to make steam (as water does when it boils)
3 moss: a very small green plant that grows on wet earth or rocks
3 crevice: a narrow crack in the surface of a rock
4 to drench: to make very wet
4 moisture: very small drops of water in the air or on a surface
6 veranda: a raised area at the front or side of a building, often made of wood
6 vegetation: plants that are found in a particular area
7 lush: very green and healthy (plants)
20 peony: a plant with big red, pink or white flowers
24 stalk: the part of a plant that supports the leaves and flowers
25 stem: the central part of a plant that comes up from the ground
41 ravine: a deep, narrow valley with steep sides
44 disdainfully: in a way that shows you do not value or respect something or someone
49 slippery: wet and smooth, making it hard to keep your balance
51 haze: heat or smoke in the air that makes it difficult to see clearly
53 amiably: in a pleasant and friendly way
55 insidiously: in an unpleasant, secretive way
62 promontory: a long, narrow area of land that sticks out into the sea
63 fainter: less strong, less noticeable
66 seaweed: a plant that grows in the sea
66 fringe: the edge of something (like the hair that hangs over the forehead)
66 to sway: to move from side to side

It was an early, very warm morning in July, and it had rained during the night. The bare granite steamed, the moss and crevices were drenched with moisture, and all the colours everywhere had deepened. Below the veranda, the vegetation in the morning shade was like a rainforest of lush, evil leaves and flowers, which she had to be careful not to break as she searched. She held one hand in front of her mouth and was constantly afraid of losing her balance.

"What are you doing?" asked little Sophia.

"Nothing," her grandmother answered. "That is to say," she added angrily, "I'm looking for my false teeth."

The child came down from the veranda. "Where did you lose them?" she asked.

"Here," said her grandmother. "I was standing right there and they fell somewhere in the peonies." They looked together.

"Let me," Sophia said. "You can hardly walk. Move over."

She dived beneath the flowering roof of the garden and crept among green stalks and stems. It was pretty mysterious down on the soft black earth. And there were the teeth, white and pink, a whole mouthful of old teeth.

"I've got them!" the child cried, and stood up. "Put them in."

"But you can't watch," Grandmother said. "That's private."

"I want to watch," she said.

So Grandmother put the teeth in, with a smacking noise. They went in very easily. It had really hardly been worth mentioning.

"When are you going to die?" the child asked.

And Grandmother answered, "Soon. But that is not the least concern of yours."

"Why?" her grandchild asked.

She didn't answer. She walked out on the rock and on towards the ravine.

"We're not allowed out there!" Sophia screamed.

"I know," the old woman answered disdainfully. "Your father won't let either one of us go out to the ravine, but we're going anyway, because your father is asleep and he won't know."

They walked across the granite. The moss was slippery. The sun had come up a good way now, and everything was steaming. The whole island was covered with a bright haze. It was very pretty.

"Will they dig a hole?" asked the child amiably.

"Yes," she said. "A big hole." And she added, insidiously, "Big enough for all of us."

"How come?" the child asked.

They walked on towards the point.

"I've never been this far before," Sophia said. "Have you?"

"No," her grandmother said.

They walked all the way out onto the little promontory, where the rock descended into the water in terraces that became fainter and fainter until there was total darkness. Each step down was edged with a light green seaweed fringe that swayed back and forth, with the movement of the sea.

Speaking

3 **Work in groups. Discuss what you think is going to happen next.**

4 Read and listen to the rest of Chapter 1. Did you guess what would happen?

"I want to go swimming," the child said. She waited for opposition, but none came. So she took off her clothes, slowly and nervously. She glanced at her grandmother – you can't depend on people who just let things happen. She put her legs in the water.

"It's cold," she said.

"Of course it's cold," the old woman said, her thoughts somewhere else. "What did you expect?"

The child slid in up to her waist and waited anxiously.

"Swim," her grandmother said. "You can swim."

It's deep, Sophia thought. She forgets I've never swum in deep water unless somebody was with me. And she climbed out again and sat down on the rock.

"It's going to be a nice day today," she declared.

The sun had climbed higher. The whole island, and the sea, were glistening. The air seemed very light.

"I can dive," Sophia said. "Do you know what it feels like when you dive?"

"Of course I do," her grandmother said. "You let go of everything and get ready and just dive. You can feel the seaweed against your legs. It's brown, and the water's clear, lighter towards the top with lots of bubbles. And you glide. You hold your breath and glide and turn and come up, let yourself rise and breathe out. And then you float. Just float."

"And all the time with your eyes open," Sophia said.

"Naturally. People don't dive with their eyes shut."

"Do you believe I can dive without me showing you?" the child asked.

"Yes, of course," Grandmother said. "Now get dressed. We can get back before he wakes up."

The first weariness came closer. When we get home, she thought, when we get back I think I'll take a little nap. And I must remember to tell him this child is still afraid of deep water.

[1] **opposition:** strong disagreement

[8] **to slide:** (past tense: *slid*) to move smoothly and continuously over a surface

[15] **to glisten:** to shine by reflecting light from a wet or smooth surface

[21] **to glide:** to move easily and without stopping

[28] **weariness:** tiredness (especially after working hard for a long time)

[29] **nap:** a short sleep

5 Work in pairs or small groups. What is going on in the minds of Sophia and her grandmother here? Go through the extract, commenting on what each of them says.

6 You have now read the first chapter of *The Summer Book*. There are 22 chapters in the book. Each has a title: 'Moonlight', 'The Cat', 'The Cave', 'The Tent', 'The Visitor', etc. Imagine another scene featuring Sophia and her grandmother and write it.

Check your progress

General knowledge quiz

1 In which country are Mantua and Verona?

2 Who was Andrea Mantegna?

3 What is a fresco?

4 What is an amphitheatre?

5 Shakespeare wrote two plays set in Verona. Name one of them.

6 Where is Agadir?

7 South Africa is between two oceans, the Atlantic and which other ocean?

8 It's an island country 30 km south-east of India. It's called Sri ... .

9 What do you call this kind of pattern?

10 Where was the writer and artist Tove Jansson born and what was her first language?

Vocabulary

Holidays

1 **How many compound nouns can you make by combining words from the two columns?**

boat	court
day	park
ice	pool
roller	skating
sightseeing	skiing
swimming	sports
tennis	tour
theme	trip
water	
a boat trip	***a day trip***

Tourism

2 **Complete each of these sentences with a word from the box. Then write another sentence to show its meaning.**

accommodation	litter	monitor
souvenir	wildlife	

a The volunteers in the conservation area ***monitor*** the elephants carefully. ***They check them every day.***

b There are signs everywhere saying, 'Please don't drop ....'.

c I know there are hotels near the beach, but are there any other types of ....?

d It's nice to take home a .... from your holiday.

e The thing that surprised me about our holiday in Madagascar was the variety of ....

Use of English

1 Each of these sentences contains a multi-word verb, but one word is missing. What is it?

a My parents always take two weeks *off* during the summer, so that we can go on holiday.

b I'm really looking forward .... hearing from you.

c I saw some of my friends from primary school the other day. It was good to catch up .... them.

d The holiday got .... to a bad start, I'm afraid.

e The film started at 7 but of course Jose turned .... at 7.30.

2 Choose the right option.

a We didn't need to get a taxi from the airport because we ***were picked up / picked up*** by my aunt.

b We couldn't go into the gym because it ***was being used / was using*** for exams.

c ***Did you hear / Were you hearing*** the thunder last night?

d Sorry I couldn't talk when you phoned. I ***was helping / helped*** to prepare the dinner.

3 Complete the compound adjectives in this account.

When you're on holiday, be open- *minded* [1]. Talk to people, ask them what you should see and do. It's easy to talk to people if you stay at a family-........... [2] hotel and buy a few souvenirs at a market. My grandmother collects hand........... [3] pottery, so I always buy her something. She was so pleased with the bowl I gave her last year. She said it was the colour of midnight – a very, very .... [4] blue. Last year, we also brought back some locally .... [5] olive oil for our neighbours.

4 Complete the adjectives with the correct ending: *-ed* or *-ing*.

a Why are tigers an endanger...... species?

b We really enjoyed our volunteering holiday. It was so reward......

c Rome was great but our hotel was a bit disappoint......

d Since my holiday in Jordan, I'm much more interest...... in history.

e It's excit...... to discover new places.

Summary checklist

I can

- ☐ talk about past and future holidays.
- ☐ plan a holiday for friends visiting my country.
- ☐ give arguments for and against in a debate on tourism.
- ☐ write a travel blog.
- ☐ give a presentation about a volunteer holiday and a school trip.
- ☐ write a report of a school trip.
- ☐ read and understand a description of a summer holiday.

4 Science

In this unit you will…

- **learn** about how we see colours
- **learn** about the history of diseases and **talk** about developments in medical science
- **listen to** a conversation about DNA and genetics
- **read** about a young Kenyan's invention for protecting livestock and wildlife
- **differentiate** between fact and opinion in texts about endangered species
- **listen to**, **understand** and **exchange** opinions about zoos
- **write** a short essay giving your views about zoos
- **research** and **present** the life of a medical pioneer
- **give** a performance of a poem.

Getting started

"Why is science important in our lives?"

Watch this!

4.1 The science of colour

In this lesson you will...

- learn about how we see colours
- describe colours and shades of colour.

- **Which colours do you think of for each of these words: warm, cold, happy, depressed, enthusiastic, energetic, calm?**

Reading

1 **Read the text. Do all humans and animals see colour in the same way?**

Research shows that colour really does affect our minds and bodies. The colour blue helps us to feel calm. Red, on the other hand, can make us feel angry. Football teams seem to play better when wearing red. They are more likely to win matches than those wearing other colours.

After analysing recent sales of works of art, a leading expert concluded that pictures with red in them fetch higher prices than those without.

Colour is how our eyes interpret light. It is the way our brain perceives mixtures of different light wavelengths falling on the retina of the eyes. Human vision is trichromatic – we have three different colour receptors (cones) in our eyes. These receptors are red, green and blue, and each is designed to pick up different wavelengths of light. People who are colour-blind detect fewer colours as one type of receptor is not working properly.

There are people who are tetrachromatic, which means they have an extra cone type in their eyes. The average person can see approximately one million colours, whereas people who have tetrachromatic vision can see 99 million.

Birds are also tetrachromatic – they have four colour receptors and see things that we see as red as many different shades of colour. This is very useful for them while searching for food.

2 **Read the text again and answer the questions using the words in the vocabulary box to help you.**

colour-blind	cone	light	receptor	retina	shade (of colour)

a Why do we not see colours at night? What is necessary for us to see colours?

b Which part of the eye receives light wavelengths?

c What are the colour receptors in your eyes called?

d How do you describe someone who can't see certain colours?

e What is the difference between being trichromatic and tetrachromatic?

f Why does being tetrachromatic help birds when they're looking for food?

3 Complete these questions using one of the conjunctions from the box. Then ask and answer them with a partner.

after	before	when	while

a Do you understand more about how birds find food .... learning that they are tetrachromatic?

b Why do you think designers and fashion experts know what to look for .... choosing colours that go well together?

c To prepare for a visit to an art exhibition, is it helpful to read about the artist .... seeing their work?

d Did you see anything colourful .... walking to school this morning? What was it?

e Do you think you are more aware of colour .... learning about how we see it? How has this changed the way you think about colours?

Use of English
Conjunctions

Conjunctions are words that join clauses together in a sentence. Some conjunctions can be followed by *-ing* forms.

Find the following conjunctions in the text. What are the *-ing* forms that follow them?

- when
- after
- while

Listening

20

4 Listen to a conversation between two friends. What is it about?

5 Listen again. Then answer the questions.

a How many words are commonly used in English to describe colours?

b What is different about Russian, Greek and Turkish?

c Why do the two friends decide to do an experiment?

d What is the experiment and what does it show?

Speaking tip

You can describe shades of colour like this:

- dark (or deep) blue, green, red, orange, yellow
- light (or pale) pink, blue, green, grey, orange, brown
- mix of colours: yellowish-brown, greyish-white, reddish-brown

Speaking

6 Work in small groups. Discuss the colours in this picture.

How would you describe the colours in this picture?
I'd say the house on the left is (pale orange).
I'd describe that colour as (yellowish-brown).

4.2 Deadly diseases

In this lesson you will…

- learn about the history of diseases
- talk about developments in medical science.

- **Do people have better health now than a hundred years ago? Why?**

Reading

1 **Read the text. How does it relate to our health today?**

2 **Answer these questions.**

a An epidemic is a large number of cases of disease that happen at the same time. What is a pandemic?

b When and why is quarantine necessary?

c What is a fatal disease?

d What was Edward Jenner's experiment?

e Why do fewer people die from influenza and tuberculosis now than a hundred years ago?

f Why is smallpox no longer a danger?

3 **Make these sentences passive.**

a They vaccinate most children against diseases such as measles and polio.

Most children are vaccinated against diseases such as measles and polio.

b They discovered a link between contaminated water and cholera.

A link was discovered between contaminated water and cholera.

c People use quarantine to control the spread of dangerous diseases.

d A flu pandemic killed millions of people between 1918 and 1920.

e Scientists developed vaccines to give people immunity to flu.

Key words: Medical science

Infection and disease
cholera
COVID-19
influenza (flu)
MERS
pandemic
plague
SARS
smallpox
tuberculosis (TB)
typhoid

Prevention and treatment
(good) sanitation
antibiotic
quarantine
vaccination, vaccine

Use of English Present and past simple passive

The passive is formed with part of the verb **be** + a **past participle**.

*Most people **are vaccinated** in childhood against diseases such as measles, rubella, diphtheria, tetanus and polio.*

*An estimated 75 to 200 million people **were killed** by the plague in Asia and Europe between 1321 and 1353.*

The plague known as the Black Death was one of the worst pandemics in human history. An estimated 75 to 200 million people were killed by the disease in Asia and Europe between 1321 and 1353. It spread from one country to another via trading routes over land such as the Silk Road and also by sea. It recurred throughout the 14th to the 18th centuries. It spread rapidly from person to person, usually causing death within three days. Nobody knew what the disease was caused by nor how to cure or prevent it. However, during the 17th century, quarantine was beginning to be used: people had to stay inside their houses for 40 days if a member of the household had the disease.

Smallpox, another fatal disease, spread throughout Asia, Europe, Africa and the Americas from the 6th to the 18th centuries, due to increasing trade and exploration.

In 1796, Edward Jenner, an English doctor, noticed that milkmaids (girls who looked after cows) got cowpox, a disease similar to smallpox, but they didn't get smallpox. He inoculated an eight-year-old boy with cowpox by exposing him to the infection. Two months later, Jenner inoculated the boy with smallpox. The boy didn't get the disease. In 1798, Jenner published the results of his work, calling the process 'vaccination'. By 1853, vaccination against smallpox had become compulsory in Britain. Just over a century later, in 1980, the World Health Organization declared that smallpox had been eradicated.

During the 19th century, however, there were many other serious health problems. Many people suffered from diseases such as cholera, tuberculosis and typhoid. Between 1817 and 1917, cholera epidemics killed around 38 million people. Eventually, a link between cholera (a bacterial infection) and contaminated water was discovered. Providing clean water and sewers reduced cases of the illness considerably.

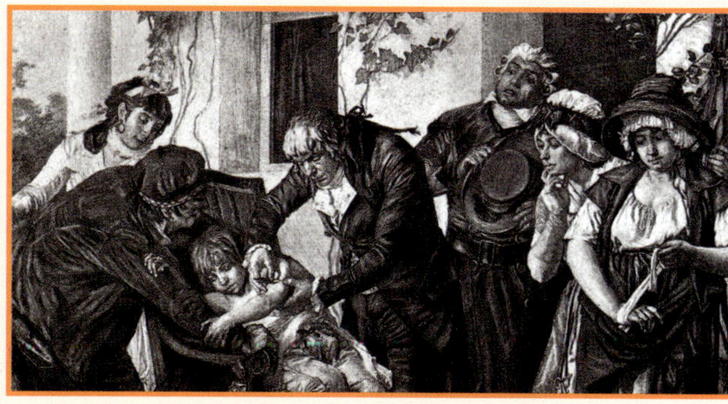

Edward Jenner vaccinates a boy with cowpox to provide immunity against smallpox, 1796

In the 20th century, diseases such as influenza and tuberculosis were widespread. The 1918 flu pandemic killed between 3 and 5 per cent of the world's population between 1918 and 1920. Fortunately, flu vaccines were developed in the 1930s. Then, in the 1950s, more progress was made when the antibiotic streptomycin was found to be effective in the treatment of tuberculosis.

In the 21st century, most people are vaccinated in childhood against diseases such as measles, rubella, diphtheria, tetanus and polio. However, new viral diseases such as SARS (Severe Acute Respiratory Syndrome), MERS (Middle East Respiratory Syndrome) and COVID-19 continue to challenge medical science.

Speaking

4 **Work in small groups. Discuss the following questions.**

- a Is learning about the history of diseases relevant to us today? Why?
- b What comparisons are there between diseases in the 14th century and today's health issues?
- c Why is vaccination important for you and for others?
- d How can scientific research improve health?

4.3 What makes us the same? What makes us different?

In this lesson you will...

- listen to a conversation about DNA and genetics
- use the present perfect continuous to talk about what you've been learning in science.

- **Do any members of your family look alike? Do they have the same hair and eye colour? What other features make them look similar?**

Listening

21 **1** **Listen to the conversation. Have Amber and her brother Rian just had the same science lesson? How do you know?**

Vocabulary

2 **Match the words to their definitions.**

Words		Definitions
DNA	a	being the only one of its kind, so there is no other that is the same
gene	b	deoxyribonucleic acid, a chemical which is present in all living organisms
genetics	c	part of a cell that controls particular characteristics
fingerprints	d	the complete set of DNA for a human, including all of its genes
unique	e	the mark made by a person's fingertips which has a unique pattern of lines
human genome	f	the study of genes and inherited characteristics

3 **Work in pairs. Answer the questions. Listen again if you need to.**

a How much of everyone's DNA is the same?
b What kind of differences in people do genes control?
c Why is DNA useful for solving crimes?
d What did the experiment about fingerprints show the students?
e What has Rian been learning about in science?

Use of English Present perfect continuous

We use the **present perfect continuous** to talk about events or situations that started in the past and have continued up until now.

have / has + been + -ing

***We've** been doing some really interesting things in science this week.*

Read the following sentences. Why is the present perfect continuous used in the first sentence and the past simple in the second sentence?

***We've** been learning about DNA, genetics and the human genome.*
*Today, **we did** an experiment that was really fun and a bit messy!*

We also use the present perfect continuous for actions that have just happened and have visible results.

***They've** been playing football.*

4 **Prepare a short talk about what you've been doing in science and in other subjects this week. Read what you've written to your partner. Can you add any more information?**

This week, we've been learning about …

We've been finding out …

In PE we've been playing …

Today we've been …

4.4 Live and let live

In this lesson you will...

- read about a young Kenyan's invention
- use the present perfect active and passive.

- **What sort of problems do you think farmers in East Africa have?**

Reading

1 **Read the text below. What problem did Richard Turere's family have on their farm?**

Richard Turere is a Kenyan Maasai herder. He lives with his family, who are farmers, near the Nairobi National Park. Richard looks after the family's cattle but he is also an inventor and has his own company, Lion Lights.

From the age of nine, Richard has been responsible for looking after the family's livestock – their cows, goats and sheep. Their farm is on the edge of the Nairobi National Park. The park is full of rhinos, giraffes, zebras, buffalo and lions. The lions would come at night and feed on the cattle while the family were sleeping.

At the age of 11, Richard came up with an idea for keeping the lions away. One night, as he was walking around with a torch keeping watch over the animals, he noticed something. He noticed that the lions were scared of the moving light. Lions are naturally afraid of people, and Richard realised that the lions linked the moving torchlight with people, so they stayed away. Using some bulbs and wires, Richard set up a series of flashing lights to give the impression that people were walking around the land where the animals were kept. The lions didn't come near. Soon other farmers nearby were using his 'lion lights'.

Many lions have been killed by farmers trying to protect their animals, but now the lion lights have helped the farmers and they have also helped to save the lions. They have been installed in 750 farms in the local community.

Richard's invention has made him famous. It has been adopted by farmers to protect their animals from predators such as cheetahs and leopards as well as lions. The lights also protect their crops from elephants. All of these animals are endangered species. According to the Kenyan Wildlife Service, there are only around 1,700 lions left in the wild in Kenya. Now the farmers can live with the lions without any problems.

Vocabulary

2 **Answer the questions.**

a What is a 'herder'?
b Why is living near the Nairobi National Park a problem for Richard Turere's family and for other farmers?
c What gave Richard the idea that lights could solve the problem?
d Why do the lion lights help to protect wildlife as well as farm animals?
e The lion lights not only help farmers protect their animals. In what other way are they useful?

22

3 **Listen to this extract from the programme *Clever ideas that have changed the world*. Was the programme recorded when Richard was a child or when he was a young adult? How do you know?**

4 **Work in pairs. What extra information does the extract give you about Richard?**

Use of English Present perfect active and passive

Use the **present perfect** for situations continuing up to now and for things that have happened, but are not linked to a specific past time.

Active
have / has present tense + past participle
*The lion lights **have helped** the farmers.*
*Richard's invention **has made** him famous.*

Passive
have / has been + past participle
*Many lions **have been killed** by farmers trying to protect their animals.*
*Richard's invention **has been adopted** by farmers to protect their animals.*

5 **Complete the sentences using the verbs in brackets in the present perfect passive.**

a All of Richard's inventions ***have been made*** from simple things and old appliances. (*make*)
b Richard .... to look after his family's livestock since he was nine years old. (*expect*)
c Crops .... from elephants by Richard's lion lights. (*protect*)
d The lives of both the farm animals and the lions ...., thanks to Richard's invention. (*save*)
e The lion lights .... by environmentalists because they are powered by solar energy and they protect wildlife. (*welcome*)

Speaking

6 **Work in small groups. Discuss these questions.**

a What are the advantages of Richard's invention?
b Why is this lesson called 'Live and let live'?

4.5 The circle of life

In this lesson you will...

- read two texts about endangered species and differentiate between fact and opinion.

Key words: Environmental science

extinct
habitat loss
herbivore
hunting
in captivity
interdependent
in the wild
poacher
pollinator
prey

- **How many ways can you think of in which we are dependent on each other? What else do we depend on?**

Reading

1 **Read these two articles. They are on the same topic. How are they different?**

Article A

An animal or plant species is declared extinct when it has not been seen for many years. The rate of extinction is now increasing quickly. Between 30% and 50% of all species could become extinct by 2050. The disappearance of so many animals, insects and plants is due mainly to human activity, through habitat loss, pollution and climate change. Towns and cities are expanding into rural areas, which means that animals don't have enough food, water and shelter. Plastics and chemicals such as pesticides contaminate the soil. Air, water, noise and light pollution also harm wildlife and the ecosystem.

Hunting reduces the number of animals in the wild. People pay to kill wildlife such as elephants, lions and other big cats. According to the African Wildlife Association, Africa's lion population has decreased in size by approximately 42% in the past 20 years. Fish, reptiles, spiders, birds and mammals are captured and sold as pets; poachers kill wild animals to sell their body parts. Every year, according to the National Geographic Society, poachers take more than 38 million animals from Brazil. Most are birds, which become pets.

Animal and plant life are interdependent. We rely on bees, butterflies and other pollinators to make plants grow, to feed herbivores as well as humans. In the wild, the reduction in herbivores means that predators whose prey are animals like deer, zebra and antelope don't have enough food. Some animals and insects are particularly dependent on each other: there are birds that feed on the insects that live on a hippopotamus. If hippos become extinct, so do the birds. A study by researchers at Oregon State University concluded that about 60% of large herbivores are in danger of extinction.

Fortunately, conservation programmes are making progress. For example, in 1985, there were fewer than 100 rhinos left in the wild. Now, there are around 21,000. Numbers of giant pandas have also increased with around 1800 currently living in the wild and around 300 in captivity. Consequently, they are considered to be 'vulnerable' rather than 'endangered'.

Article B

Extinction is a natural process. Take the example of the dodo. It simply wasn't strong enough to survive. Ask people to name a species that has become extinct and it's always the dodo. But the dodo became extinct four centuries ago.

We are told that loss of habitat means that animals find it hard to survive. Animals and plants adapt to new surroundings: foxes learn to live in cities, camels and cactus plants survive in the desert, polar bears live in the Arctic. Of course, there are always programmes on TV that show us how the ice is melting and the polar bears are finding it hard to survive, and warning of the dangers of oil and gas exploration destroying their habitat. But there is no reason why you can't use the Arctic for oil and gas and still leave plenty of space for bears. The people who want to stop this are just anti-big business. They just want to stop those of us who work hard to provide oil and gas for the people of this world. The Arctic is a big place. There's enough room for human beings and animals. People also claim that we are responsible for climate change. They seem to forget that climate change has been happening for millions of years. Yes, the Earth is getting warmer, but we just have to get used to it.

2 **Read the articles again and find the words and phrases in the environmental science key words box. Work with a partner to say what they mean.**

A: *Extinct. That's when an animal disappears for ever.*

3 **Read the dictionary definitions of the words *objective* and *biased*, then answer the questions about the articles.**

a Is one article more objective than the other? Support your answer with examples.

b Is one article biased? What makes you think this?

c Reread Article B. What do we learn about the writer?

objective: influenced only by facts and not by feelings

biased: supporting or opposing a particular person or things in an unfair way, by allowing personal opinions to influence your judgement

Speaking

4 **You have been asked to take part in a television debate on the effect that towns and cities can have on the natural world. Divide the class into two groups.**

- Group A argues that we must stop the spread of towns and cities because it reduces the size of natural habitats for plants and animals (including insects).
- Group B argues that we have to build homes for people and places for them to work. This means expanding existing towns and cities.

4.6 Views on zoos

In this lesson you will...

- listen to, understand and exchange opinions about zoos
- use verbs followed by prepositions.

- **Why do zoos exist?**

Vocabulary

1 **You will hear these words and phrases in the interview in Exercise 2. To prepare, match the words to the definitions.**

enclosure
instinct
keeper
breed
genetic diversity
cage
wildlife park
release (into the wild)

a to allow animals bred in captivity to live in freedom in their natural habitat
b variety of genetic characteristics in a species
c the natural way an animal behaves
d a large park where wildlife live in captivity
e a structure of bars or wires in which animals are kept
f an area surrounded by a fence in which animals are kept
g to reproduce
h a person who looks after animals in a zoo

Listening

23

2 **Listen to six people talking about zoos. Who is in favour of zoos? Who is against them? Write 'for' or 'against' for each person.**

a Amir *against*
b Isla
c Huyen
d Onel
e Shashi
f Kareem

3 **Listen again. Which person gives each of these opinions?**

a Going to the zoo is a great day out for families.
b If people want to see wild animals, they should watch wildlife programmes on TV.
c It goes against wild animals' natural instincts to be kept in cages or enclosures.

A reptile responds to a young visitor at the zoo

d Seeing animals in a zoo helps people to identify with and care about wildlife.
e Zoos breed endangered species and release them into the wild.
f Taking animals from the wild reduces genetic diversity.

Use of English Dependent prepositions following verbs

There are no rules about which prepositions follow certain verbs. It's best to learn and use them as often as you can.

Copy and complete the chart when you've done Exercise 4.

in	from	of	on	to	with
believe in	***suffer from***	die of		belong to	agree with
succeed in			concentrate on		compare with
			rely on		

4 **Complete these sentences with the correct prepositions. Then put each verb + preposition in the correct place in the Use of English box.**

a I think that animals in zoos suffer ***from*** stress and boredom.
b There are zoos that specialise .... breeding animals, such as the giant panda, in captivity.
c In zoos and wildlife parks, endangered species can be protected .... dangers such as habitat loss and being killed by poachers and hunters.
d Breeding endangered species in zoos to release into the wild can save them .... extinction.
e I don't agree .... people who say that zoos can provide a good environment for animals.
f I don't approve .... any species being taken from the wild.
g Zoos are a good way of introducing people .... the amazing variety of species.
h But you should also listen .... the experts who say that taking animals from the wild reduces genetic diversity.
i The survival of many species in the wild will depend .... people protecting their habitats.

Speaking

5 **Work in small groups. Discuss these questions.**

a Do you approve of animals being kept in zoos?
b What do zoos and wildlife parks succeed in doing?

4.7 Improve your writing

In this lesson you will...

- write an essay giving your views about zoos.

1 **Read the model essay on the opposite page. Answer the questions.**

Paragraph 1 (Introduction)

a Which words and phrases in the opening sentence tell you what the writer thinks about animals?

b Why do you think the writer asks a question in the second sentence? Is this a good idea at the beginning of an essay?

Paragraph 2

c In your opinion, which of the reasons in favour of zoos provides the strongest argument for them?

d Why does the writer give examples about species bred in captivity?

Paragraph 3

e What is the purpose of the second sentence?

f Which parts of the third and fourth sentences give opinions rather than facts?

Paragraph 4 (Conclusion)

g What is the writer's answer to the question "Are you for or against zoos"?

2 **Write a plan for your essay.**

- Introduce the topic of your argument.
- Give reasons in favour of zoos.
- Give reasons against zoos.
- Conclude by summarising the main points of your argument. Make your overall opinion clear.

3 **Brainstorm ideas for and against zoos. Look back at Lesson 4.6 to help you. Make notes under two headings:**

For	*Against*
fun for children	*animals in captivity … bored and stressed*

Writing tip

Connectives are words that link ideas within a text. Here are some examples you can use.

To list or add ideas:

First, To start, In the first place… ; Second, In addition, Furthermore … ; Third, Finally

To introduce examples or give reasons:

For example, such as, like, therefore, for this reason, because

To link contrasting ideas:

However, but, although, while … whereas

To add emphasis:

not only … but also …

To conclude:

In conclusion, To conclude, To sum up

4 Write a first draft of your essay.

- Make sure you link your ideas so that the meaning of your argument is clear. Check that you have followed all the points in Exercise 2.
- Check the spelling, grammar and punctuation.
- Show your draft to another student and ask for comments and suggestions.

5 Write a final version of your essay.

Are you for or against zoos?

Start with a sentence to draw the reader into the topic.

Introduce the main points of your argument.

From the smallest insect to the largest mammal, animals are essential to life on Earth, so it is not surprising that humans find them fascinating. However, is it right to take animals from the wild and keep them in captivity in zoos and wildlife parks or should all wild animals live in freedom?

Give reasons in support of zoos.

Use connectives to link your ideas.

Do research to find evidence to support your views and include it.

Children can learn about animals from books and films but seeing them in real life is much more exciting and helps to encourage enthusiasm for knowing about the natural world. A visit to the zoo is not only an enjoyable experience but it is also educational because visitors learn about the different species and what they need to survive. In addition, zoos and wildlife parks can protect animals from dangers that threaten their survival in the wild. Zoos have also succeeded in breeding animals that are endangered species, such as the giant panda, the Arabian oryx and the golden lion tamarin.

Give reasons against zoos.

However, when animals are kept in a zoo or even in a wildlife park, they are not free to live as they would in the wild. For example, a lion in a zoo doesn't need to hunt for its prey and it cannot leave its enclosure, so it is not a natural way of life for a wild animal. Cages and enclosures are necessary in order to keep visitors safe but they are a prison for the animals. While some species adapt well and live happily in captivity, others appear bored, stressed and unhappy.

Summarise the main points of the argument in your conclusion.

Finish by saying whether you are for or against zoos and explain why.

Zoos and wildlife parks that provide good conditions for their animals are a pleasure to visit and help towards the survival of many species. Nevertheless, it does not seem right for humans to keep animals in captivity, particularly when it is possible to find out about wildlife and see them in their natural environment in films and in wildlife programmes on TV.

4.8 Project challenge

Project 1: A species in danger of extinction

You are going to make a fact file about an animal species in danger of extinction.

1. Work in groups. First do some research to find out about some endangered species. Select one you think is interesting.
2. Tell your group about the animal you have selected, giving the reasons for your choice. The group discusses all the suggestions and then makes a collective decision about which species to present on the fact file.
3. Research and write notes about the animal. Look at the notes below about the Amur leopard to help you.
4. Find a photo of the animal you have chosen. Write a caption for it to use as the title for your fact file.
5. Write your notes on the fact file.
6. Give a presentation to the class based on your fact file. Explain why you have chosen to feature this species.

The world's rarest wild cat

Name:
Amur leopard

Scientific name: *Panthera pardus orientalis*

Endangered status: critically endangered

Population: (estimated) 84 individuals

Habitats: forests in the east of Russia

Features: solitary, fast, strong

Lifespan: 10–15 years in the wild, up to 20 years in captivity

Major threat: illegal wildlife trade

Poachers kill the leopards in order to sell their beautiful spotted fur. Habitat loss and lack of prey are also a problem.

Positive steps: stop poaching, increase prey population (deer, wild boar), protect habitat

Good news:
Russia created a new protected area for the Amur leopards in 2012. It's called 'Land of the Leopard National Park'.

- What did you like most about doing this project?
- What did you learn about working as part of a team?

Project 2: A medical pioneer

You are going to prepare and give a three-minute speech about Edward Jenner, Marie Curie, Louis Pasteur, Al-Zahrawi, Uğur Şahin and Özlem Türeci, or another important scientist who has made a difference to world health.

1 Work in groups. Discuss who you will choose as the subject of your speech.

2 Find out about the life and achievements of the scientist you have chosen.

Divide the following research questions among the members of the group:

- Where and when did the scientist live?
- What did he / she discover?
- How was the discovery received at the time?
- How did the discovery help people?

Uğur Şahin and Özlem Türeci, the research scientists who developed the Pfizer vaccine against COVID-19

3 Each member of the group writes their section of the speech, using the information they have found.

4 Take turns to read out what you have written. The rest of the group listens and suggests any corrections to the grammar and pronunciation.

5 Make notes giving the key information for your section, so that you can give your part of the speech without reading it.

6 Practise giving your speech from your notes.

7 Give your speech. If you are feeling nervous, take a few deep breaths and relax first. Look at the audience as you speak – don't look down. Speak slowly and calmly. Smile.

8 Ask for comments and questions from your audience.

- What was the most useful or interesting aspect of doing this project?
- How did it affect the way you feel about speaking in public?

4.9 Poetry

The poem on the opposite page is based on an ancient Greek fable. A fable is a short story, often with animals as characters, that has a 'moral' – a lesson about how people should or shouldn't behave.

24

1 Read and listen to the poem. What is the moral of the story it tells? Find one line in the poem which gives the moral.

2 Work in pairs. Ask and answer these questions.

Student A: Ask Student B	Student B: Ask Student A
a How would you describe the character of the hare? Give examples to show what you mean.	a How would you describe the character of the tortoise? Give examples to show what you mean.
b In lines 1 to 35, which words rhyme?	b In lines 36 to 61, which words rhyme?
c What do you notice about lines 25 to 35, describing the hare running? (Compare them with the lines describing the tortoise.)	c What do you notice about lines 21 to 24 and lines 42 to 45, describing the tortoise? (Compare them with the lines describing the hare.)
d Summarise what happens in lines 1 to 35.	d Summarise what happens in lines 36 to 61.

3 Take turns to read a line each, around the class. Depending on the size of the class, you may have several lines to read.

- Practise saying your lines. Your teacher will help with pronunciation.
- Give a performance of the poem.

4 Close your books and give a performance of the poem!

5 Write another verse for 'Tortoise and Hare Race'. Think of what the tortoise and the hare might have said to each other after the race.

[2] No wonder: It's not surprising
[4] snort: a loud sound made by breathing out through your nose (here, showing that Tortoise is annoyed)
[7] springy: moving up and down quickly and energetically
[8] ping: to move quickly and suddenly with a short ringing sound
[11] besides: in addition, also
[14] fairly: in a fair way, so that neither has an advantage
[19] jeer: to laugh at in an unkind way
[21] get away: to leave, to start a journey
[22] jog: to run at a slow, steady speed
[39] tick away: to make a continual ticking noise, like a mechanical clock
[42] creep up: to approach slowly and quietly
[44] was in sight: 1 could be seen; 2 would happen soon
[45] boast: to tell other people proudly about what you have done, expecting them to admire you
[47] shock: an unpleasant surprise
[50] leap: jump high into the air
[58] ahead: in front
[60] despite: used to say that something is true even though something else might have prevented it
[61] pace: the speed at which you run, walk or move

Tortoise and Hare Race

'Tortoise, you're very slow you know.
No wonder. Your legs are so short.'

'I get to where I want to go,'
said Tortoise with a snort.

Hare
was everywhere,
light and springy,
pinging past
fast,
all over the place.

'Besides I'd beat you in a race
if we were having one.'
'All right, we'll let Fox choose the place,
and see it's fairly run.'

The race began.
Off Hare ran.
'I'll probably win
before you begin,'
he jeered
as he disappeared.

And Tortoise was slow getting away
but he said as he jogged along,
'Little by little wins the day.
And Hare will get bored before long.'

Hare
was so sure
he'd be there
before
the Tortoise,
he thought
he'd take
a short break
and fell deep
asleep
in the sun.

He slept
and slept
while the minutes
kept on ticking away
through the heat of the day.

And still he slept
as Tortoise crept up and passed
on his way to the Finishing Post.
The end of the race was in sight at last.
He expected Hare there to boast.

But Hare woke
with a shock.
His body-clock
said he'd overslept.
So up he leapt
and started to run –
but there was someone
already ahead
and at this minute
about to win.
'It can't be Tortoise.'
But it was.

Yes, there ahead with Fox was Tortoise –
winner of the race
and that despite his legs' shortness
and his slow pace.

Jill Townsend

6 **Read and listen to 'The Farmer's Cat'. What do you like about it?**

7 **Work with a partner. Talk about how the poem is constructed. Then say why you think the poet wrote it.**

A: There are six verses.
B: Verse 3 is almost the same as verse 1.
A: Yes, but …
B: Verse 4 is almost the same as verse 2, but …
A: In the first four verses, the cat is watching the farmer. However, in verse 5 …
B: And in the last verse, …
A: I think the poet wanted to show that …

The Farmer's Cat
From the traditional Chinese

Out in the fields
in spring time,
the farmer's cat follows him
as he plants the seeds of corn.

The cat dances with the raindrops
and sleeps in the sun
and when autumn comes
she sees that the farmer
has a field full of corn.

Out in the fields
in spring time,
the farmer's cat follows him
as he plants the peanut seeds.

The cat dances with the raindrops
and sleeps in the sun
and when autumn comes
she sees that the farmer
has a field full of tasty peanuts.

Out in the fields
in spring time,
the farmer watches while his cat
plants rows of tiny fish.

The cat dances with the raindrops
and sleeps in the sun
and dreams that when autumn comes
she will fill her dish
with all the silver fish
that she's grown in the farmer's fields.

David Greygoose

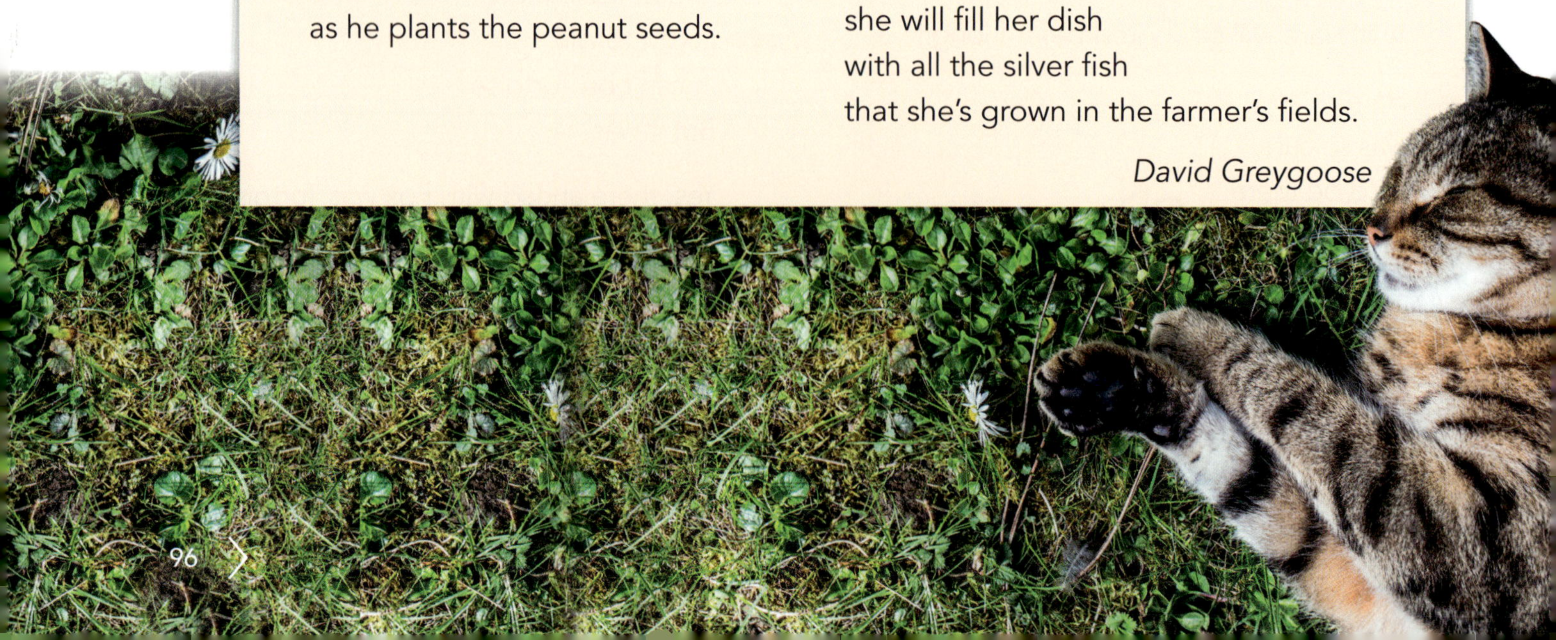

Check your progress

General knowledge quiz

1. How many colour receptors (cones) do most people have in their eyes?
2. Birds are tetrachromatic. What does this mean?

3. What was the Black Death?
4. What helped to reduce cases of cholera in towns and cities in the 19th century?
5. For which disease was the antibiotic streptomycin found to be an effective treatment?
6. Which three letters are the abbreviation for deoxyribonucleic acid?
7. Why do detectives use fingerprints to help them solve crimes?
8. In which country is the Nairobi National Park?
9. What was the dodo and what happened to it?
10. How have conservation programmes helped species such as giant pandas and rhinos?

Vocabulary

Medical science and diseases

1 **Match the medical and scientific words to their definitions.**

inoculation pandemic quarantine human genome antibiotic

a the DNA of a human
b a medicine that doctors use to treat bacterial infections such as TB
c giving a weak form of a disease, usually by injection, to protect against the disease
d a disease that affects people over a whole country or the world
e being isolated from other people to avoid spreading a disease

Wildlife

2 **Complete the sentences with the words from the list.**

herbivores extinct endangered pollinators predators prey

a When there are very few of a particular kind of animal left, they are considered …………
b When there are none of a species, it means they have become …………
c Insects like bees and butterflies are ………… They're needed to make plants grow.

d If there aren't enough plants to eat, ..., such as buffalo and antelope, don't survive.

e Herbivores are the .... for animals like cheetahs, leopards and lions.

f If the meat-eating .... don't have enough prey, their numbers are reduced.

Use of English

1 **Join these sentences using the conjunctions in brackets followed by the *-ing* form of the verb.**

a I read the article about colours. I looked at colours in a different way. (*after*)
I looked at colours in a different way after reading the article about colours.

b Birds use their ability to see many shades of red and other colours. They look for berries on plants and trees. (*while*)

c I didn't know about the plague and smallpox. I read about the history of diseases. (*before*)

2 **Complete the text by writing the verbs in present or past passive.**

There is evidence that inoculation using material infected with smallpox ***was used***[1] (*use*) in China from the 1500s. In 1661, for example, Emperor K'ang's children ......[2] (*inoculate*). Infected material taken from somebody with smallpox ......[3] (*rub*) into scratches made on children's arms. This meant that they ......[4] (*protected*) from the disease.

The development of vaccination against smallpox ......[5] (*develop*) further by Edward Jenner until eventually the disease ......[6] (*eradicate*). During the 19th and 20th centuries vaccines ......[7] (*make*) to provide immunity to tetanus, cholera, plague, typhoid and TB. Nowadays children ......[8] (*vaccinate*) to give them immunity to illnesses such as measles, mumps and rubella.

Summary checklist

I can

- [ ] describe colours, shades of colours and how we see colour.
- [ ] talk about genes and discuss developments in medical science.
- [ ] identify bias in texts about conservation and wildlife.
- [ ] write an essay giving my views about zoos.
- [ ] give a presentation on a scientific topic.
- [ ] take part in a performance of a poem.

5 Technology

In this unit you will...

- **listen to** people talking about social media and **discuss** how you use it
- **read** about the technology in homes of the future
- **take** part in a discussion about social media and digital media
- **learn** about how archaeologists used technology to make a remarkable discovery
- **discuss** what should happen to important discoveries
- **make** predictions of what life will be like in ten years' time
- **write** a report on technology in your school
- **create** a technology timeline
- **read** two extracts about the history of science.

Getting started

"Windmills and the printing press are examples of early technology. Why were they important? How many other examples of early technology can you think of?"

Watch this!

5.1 Social media and you

In this lesson you will...

- listen to people talking about social media and discuss how you use it
- use relative clauses with *which*.

- **Since you were a child, what changes have there been in the way we communicate?**

Vocabulary

1 **Use the words in the box to complete the definitions.**

emoji	hashtag	like	meme	platform
post	selfie	spam	tweet	vlogging

a A .... is a photo that you take of yourself.

b An .... is a small digital image that expresses an idea or an emotion.

c A .... is a message, an image, a video, or any item shared on social media.

d A .... is a quick way of showing that you like the content of a post.

e A .... is the # sign and is used on social media to show a message is posted as part of a longer conversation.

f A .... is a joke, a comment or an image that is copied and spreads quickly on social media.

g A .... is the type of computer system you have and the programs and apps you can use with it.

h A .... is a short comment or piece of information posted on Twitter.

i .... is a combination of two words, 'video' and 'blogging'.

j ...., also called 'junk mail', refers to messages that you have not asked for.

Listening

26 **2** **Listen to see if your answers to Exercise 1 were correct.**

27 **3** **Listen to Ameena, Yusuf and Nabila talking to a radio talk show host. How would you describe the differences between them?**

4 **Listen again. Which of the items in Exercise 1 do Ameena, her father and her grandmother mention?**

5 **Complete these sentences with *which* and your own ideas.**

- **a** Most computers now have voice recognition, …
- **b** Some students only read books on their phones, …
- **c** You have to be 13 or over to use most social media services, …
- **d** Some people think that social media is just for teenagers and young people, ...

Speaking

6 **Work in groups. You have been invited to appear on the radio programme you have just heard to discuss how you use social media. One of you should be the host. Try to use the following phrases to comment on what the previous speaker has just said.**

Which is the same for me, because …
Which surprises me, because …
Which I find strange.
Which is interesting, because …
Which is fine, but …

Use of English Relative clauses

Remember

You already know how to use *which* and *that* in relative clauses:

- to give essential, defining information
  *There's a social media platform **that / which** is good for sharing messages.*
- to give extra, non-essential information
  *Even my computer, **which** is very old now, has voice recognition.*

You can also use *which* to refer to the whole of a clause, not just the noun that goes before it.

It gives you all sorts of creative ideas,
***which** is great for making presents.*

I wouldn't be without social media,
***which** surprises a lot of my friends.*

And you can use *which* in this way to comment directly on what someone has just said:

Yusuf: *My mother and my daughter know far more about all this than I do!*
Host: ***Which** surprises me!*
Ameena: *I suppose you still type all your emails.*
Nabila: ***Which** is silly.*

5.2 The home of the future

In this lesson you will…

- read about the technology in homes of the future
- revise how to express the future and use the future passive.

- **What is your favourite gadget for the home?**

Key words: Technology

artificial intelligence (AI)
automatically
data
digital assistant
drone
the internet of things (IoT)
robotics
scan
sensor
smart technology

Reading

1 **Read the article on the opposite page. Find two sentences or phrases that could be used as captions for the pictures.**

Speaking

2 **Work with a partner. In your notebook, write down the words in the technology key words box. Close your books. How much can you remember about the home of the future? Use the words from the technology key words box as a guide.**

A: ***We'll have alarm clocks that can scan our diaries.***

3 **In your groups, exchange information about developments in technology that you have heard about or read about. Keep the conversation going with comments and questions.**

A: ***I read something about the house of the future. It said that houses will be made of bricks that can store energy – like batteries.***

B: ***That sounds interesting.***

Remember Expressing the future

Remember that you can express the future in several ways in English:

- present simple (timetables and routines)
  The meeting ***starts*** *at 8 o'clock.*
- *will* (information about the future; general predictions)
  Your smart alarm clock ***will scan*** *your diary.*
  You ***won't need*** *to do – or even say – anything.*
  Developments in robotics ***will give*** *us machines that will help with all the normal routines.*
- *going to* (plans, decisions, firm intentions; predictions based on a present situation or evidence)
  What are you ***going to have*** *for dinner tonight?*
- present continuous (personal arrangements, fixed plans)
  At the weekend, your friends ***are coming*** *for a barbecue.*

Future passive with *will*

You can use the future passive with *will* when it's not important to know who (or what) is responsible for an action:

Everything ***will be done*** *automatically.*

Your data ***will be collected****.*

If you want to say who (or what) is responsible for an action, use *by*:

The cupboards will be cleaned ***by*** *a robotic arm.*

Imagine yourself in ten years' time …

You have to get to work early tomorrow because you have a meeting. It starts at 8 o'clock. Your smart alarm clock will scan your diary and find that you have to get up earlier than usual. Your alarm will buzz at 6 a.m. and it will communicate with the kitchen so that your coffee and your breakfast are ready and waiting at 6.30.

You go to the bathroom. There's no need to tell your digital assistant to turn on the light. Voice recognition is quite old-fashioned now. Thanks to the internet of things (IoT) and artificial intelligence (AI), smart homes will be able to learn about the habits of the people who live in them, so everything will be done automatically. Developments in robotics will give us machines that will help with all the normal routines. You won't need to do – or even say – anything.

Of course, your shower will turn on automatically and the water will be at exactly the right temperature. In the bathroom of the future, health sensors in your bathroom mirror will pick up any signs that you are not well. They will also check the level of oxygen in your blood and your breathing rate. Sensors in your toothbrush will make sure you are brushing your teeth properly, and will send data to your dentist.

What are you going to have for dinner tonight? Don't worry, the robots in your kitchen will prepare it for you and your oven will have it ready on time. You won't need to do anything.

At the weekend, your friends are coming for a barbecue. What about shopping for food? Don't worry. Your fridge will place an order for the food, which will be delivered by drone tomorrow morning.

The cupboards are looking a bit dirty, but they will be cleaned by a robotic arm. So sit back and relax.

In the smart home of the future, your data will be collected, analysed and used to meet every need. Your home will learn about you: the food you like, the music you enjoy, the kind of lighting you prefer. Cameras and sensors in your fridge will check on your diet.

And so to bed …

Your smart pillow will play music to send you to sleep and will of course know the exact position you need to get a good night's sleep.

5.3 Digital media: good or bad?

In this lesson you will...

- listen to a discussion about social media and digital media generally
- take part in a discussion about social media and digital media.

- **How does communicating via social media help in everyday life? Give examples.**

Reading

1 **Read these definitions. Which words did you already know?**

to socialise: to spend time enjoying yourself with other people

empathy: the ability to understand how someone feels by imagining what it would be like to be in their situation

to chat: to talk in a friendly way, often about things that are not important

addiction: the need to do something regularly, without being able to stop

to interact: to communicate and react to what someone says or does

evidence: something that makes you believe that something is true or exists

Listening and speaking

28

2 **Listen to two interviews. The first is with Laura Wilson. The second is with Dev Sharma. What differences do you notice?**

3 **Work in small groups. Listen again. Use the words and phrases in the box to summarise what each speaker says.**

online socialising	to concentrate	family life	3D (three-dimensional) modelling program
to engage (properly)	to get distracted	to interact	different points of view
face to face	education	to message	creative writing
to develop empathy	to copy	to send a message	to publish their work
messaging	addiction	educational technology	
	screen time	evidence	

4 **In your groups, answer these questions.**

- a Who gives the most balanced view, Laura Wilson or Dev Sharma? Give reasons for your answer.
- b Which speaker gives more facts to support what they say?
- c Think of what each speaker says. What do you agree with? What do you disagree with?
- d Are there any important points that the speakers missed?
- e In Lesson 4.5, you decided whether the writer of a magazine article was 'objective' or 'biased'. What would you say about Laura Wilson and Dev Sharma?

Language tip

You can use ***do / does*** in positive sentences for emphasis:

I ***do*** *understand parents who want to limit screen time.*

Parents ***do*** *need to be much stricter.*

It ***does*** *concern me that young people will not be able to socialise face to face.*

5 **Work in groups. You have been invited to take part in the discussion 'Social media, digital media: good or bad?' One person is the interviewer. He / She must make sure that everyone has a chance to speak.**

- You can use the phrases in the box in Exercise 3.
- You can also use these phrases in your discussion:

To agree
Yes, I think so.
I'm sure it does / is.
Exactly.

To disagree
I don't think so.

To suggest that something might be true
I suppose …

- Remember that you can make a link to what someone has just said by using which:

Which is interesting, because …
Which is surprising, because …

5.4 Have a story personalised!

In this lesson you will...

- listen to a conversation about a present for a younger member of the family
- use the structure *have something done*.

- **What sort of things can you have 'personalised'? Think of T-shirts, notebooks …**

Listening

29

1 **Listen to this conversation between Maya and her friends. What are they discussing?**

2 **Listen again and answer these questions.**

a The friends make four suggestions. What are they?

b Which suggestions does Maya reject, and why?

c Which suggestion does she accept, and why?

d Think of a young child you know. Which of the suggested presents would be best for them, and why?

Remember

- Use *too* before adjectives and adverbs to mean more than is necessary, acceptable or possible.
  They're ***too*** *expensive.*
- Use *too much* and *too many* before nouns.
  He already spends ***too much time*** *looking at screens.*
  I've got ***too many photos*** *on my phone. I must delete some.*

Use of English *to have something done*

You can use *to have something done* to mean 'to cause something to be done by somebody else'. There are four examples in the conversation you heard in Exercise 1. Here is one of them.

have + object + past participle
You can ***have*** *a* ***photo made*** *into a jigsaw.*

What are the other three? One is in the past tense.

3 **Complete these sentences with a suitable past participle.**

a I have my hair ………… once a month.

b I've just had my room ………… bright yellow.

c Have you ever had your photo ………… by a professional photographer?

d We don't go to the supermarket much. We usually have our food shopping ………… .

e When my computer went wrong, I had it ………… at a local electronics shop.

Vocabulary

4 **Work in groups. Look at the ideas below for presents. Think of the people you know and decide if any of the presents would be suitable to celebrate a special occasion. Give your reasons.**

have the person's name printed on a **phone cover**, a **laptop bag** …

have someone's **initials** engraved onto a **bracelet** or a **ring**

have someone's favourite photo printed on a **mouse mat**, a **coffee mug** …

have holiday photos made into a **souvenir album**

have a **T-shirt** printed with the names of all the students in someone's class

have a **box of chocolates** delivered to someone's house

have a **song** played on the radio for someone

have a **special cake** made

I'd have a special cake made for my grandmother, because she could invite all her friends round and share it with them.

5.5 Technology meets archaeology

In this lesson you will...

- learn about how archaeologists used technology to make a remarkable discovery
- discuss what should happen to important discoveries.

Key words: Ancient history

archaeologist
early Islamic
era
Greek
Ottoman
Roman

- **Which discoveries of things from the past do you know about?**

Reading

1 **Before you read the article, look at the words in the ancient history key words box, the title of the article and the photos. What do you think the article is about? ('Globalisation' refers to countries interacting and trading internationally.)**

2 **Read the article. Were your predictions correct?**

Vocabulary

3 **Use the context to help you work out the meaning of the following words and phrases. If you are not sure, check in a dictionary.**

a a shipwreck (title of the article)
b an archaeologist (line 1)
c a fleet of ships (line 3)
d the deck of a ship (line 23)
e cargo (line 23)
f a time capsule (line 41)
g a craze (line 56)

Speaking

4 **Work in groups. Discuss these questions.**

a What does this discovery tell us about trade routes?
b What does the discovery tell us about the Ottoman Empire and its customs?
c What do you think will happen to the wrecks and the artefacts that have been discovered? What should happen to them?

[11] ground-breaking: making big and important new discoveries

[15] cutting edge: very modern and with all the newest features

[21] colossus: someone or something that is extremely big

[24] artefact: an object that was made a long time ago and is historically important

[25] porcelain: a hard, shiny, white substance that is used for making cups, plates, etc.

[33] maritime: relating to the sea

[45] spanning: including all of a particular area

[49] cosmopolitan: showing the influence of many different countries and cultures

[59] civility: polite behaviour

Mediterranean shipwrecks reveal 'birth of globalisation' in trade

A team of archaeologists has made a spectacular discovery in the eastern Mediterranean: a fleet of Greek, Roman, early Islamic and Ottoman ships that were lost about two kilometres below the waves of the Levantine Basin between the 3rd century BCE and the 19th century.

Sean Kingsley, director of the Centre for East-West Maritime Exploration and archaeologist for the Enigma Shipwrecks Project (ESP), said: 'This is truly ground-breaking, one the most incredible discoveries under the Mediterranean.'

The ESP's ambitious underwater exploration used cutting-edge remote and robotic technology to research and record the finds, some of which could rewrite history, according to the experts involved.

One of the wrecks is a 17th-century Ottoman merchant ship, described as 'an absolute colossus', which was so big that two normal-sized ships could have fitted on its deck. Its vast cargo has hundreds of artefacts from 14 cultures and civilisations, including the earliest Chinese porcelain retrieved from a Mediterranean wreck, painted jugs from Italy and peppercorns from India.

ESP says the ship reveals a previously unknown maritime silk and spice route running from China to Persia, the Red Sea and into the eastern Mediterranean.

The ship, which is thought to have sunk around 1630, while sailing between Egypt and Istanbul, is a time capsule that tells the story of the beginning of the globalised world, Kingsley said. 'The goods and belongings of the 14 cultures and civilisations discovered, spanning on one side of the globe China, India, the Arabian Gulf and the Red Sea, and to the west North Africa, Italy, Spain, Portugal and Belgium, are remarkably cosmopolitan for pre-modern shipping of any era.'

The Chinese porcelain includes 360 decorated cups, dishes and a bottle made in the kilns of Jingdezhen during the reign of Chongzhen, the last Ming emperor. The cups were designed for sipping tea, but the Ottomans adapted them for the craze then spreading across the East – coffee drinking.

Kingsley said: 'Europe may think it invented notions of civility, but the wrecked coffee cups and pots [tell a different story]. The first London coffee house only opened its doors in 1652, a century after the Levant.'

Steven Vallery, co-director of Enigma, said: 'In the Levantine Basin, the Enigma wrecks lie beyond any country's territory. All the remains were carefully recorded using a suite of digital photography, [video and other technological devices]. For science and underwater exploration, these finds are a giant leap forward.'

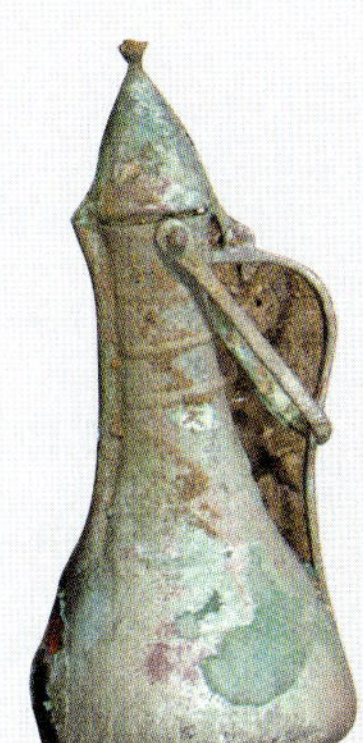

5.6 In ten years' time ...

In this lesson you will...

- make predictions of what life will be like in ten years' time
- use the future continuous.

- **Which films have you seen or which books have you read that show what life might be like in the future?**

Listening

30

1 **Listen to this conversation. What impression do you get of Jen and her father?**

2 **Use the future continuous to complete these sentences.**

a This time tomorrow, (*I / have*) a maths lesson.
I'll be having a maths lesson.

b The plane left Istanbul at 2, so (*we / arrive*) in Bodrum at about 3.20.

- c Mum (*not / come*) with us to the cinema this evening because she has to work.
- d My cousins (*not / visit*) us this year, because they're going to Australia.
- e (*we / go*) to Croatia for our holidays this year?
- f When you go to see your cousins, how long (*you / stay*)?
- g (*your parents / come*) to the end-of-term concert?

Use of English Future continuous

We use the **future continuous** to talk about things that will be in progress at a time in the future.

will + *be* + present participle

Will *you* ***be using*** *your laptop later this evening?*

We also use it to talk about planned and expected future events.

What ***will*** *you* ***be doing*** *in ten years' time?*

I'll be earning *a lot of money.* (= I expect to be earning a lot of money.)

3 Listen again. Answer these questions, using the future continuous. What does Jen say about the following?

- a voice recognition
- b work
- c self-driving cars
- d clothes
- e food

4 At one point in the conversation, Jen described this picture. What did she say? Write a caption for the picture.

Speaking

5 Work in groups. Discuss these questions.

- Do you think Jen is right in everything she says? For example, she says that people won't be using voice recognition in ten years' time? Is that true?
- What will the world be like in ten years' time?
- What will you be doing in ten years' time?

I agree with Jen about … I think we will all be using …

That's true, but I don't agree with her about …

In ten years' time we'll all be using electric vehicles.

What about aeroplanes? What sort of fuel will they be using?

I don't really know what I'll be doing in ten years' time.

But I hope I'll be …

5.7 Improve your writing

In this lesson you will...

- write a report on technology in your school.

1 **Work in groups. You are going to write a report on technology in your school for your headteacher. First, talk about the role of technology in the classroom.**

A: *I think technology is a good thing in the classroom.*

B: *In what way?*

A: *Well, reading in a foreign language is much better on an e-reader.*

C: *What do mean? Why is it better than a printed book?*

A: *Because if you don't know the meaning of a word, you just highlight it and the meaning comes up.*

C: *Oh, yes, you mean, it's quicker than looking up a word in a printed dictionary.*

A: *Yes.*

- Ask questions to find out detailed information.
- Ask questions to find out exactly what someone means.
- Check that you have understood.
- Finally, summarise what you have said.

2 **Next, write a list of the technology your school already has.**

3 **Ask your teachers how they use technology at present. Add their suggestions to your list.**

4 **Finally, do some research on new educational technology that is available. Discuss and write a list of the kind of technology you would like to have. Ask your teachers for their views.**

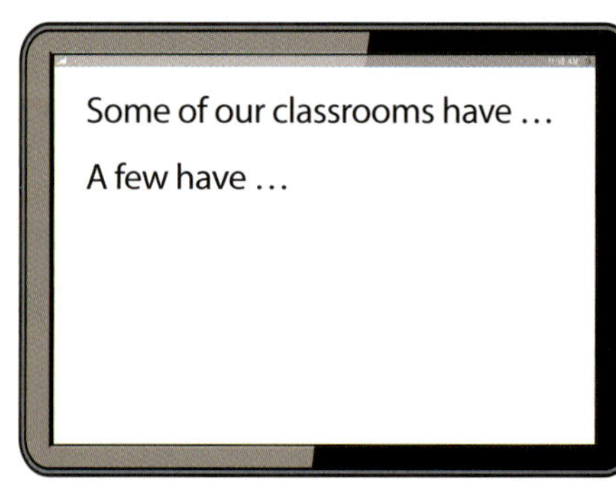

5 **Use the outline on the opposite page as a model for your report. When you have written it, check the following:**

- Have you started by saying how your report is organised?
- Have you given examples?
- Have you used connectives such as *however* and *although*?
- Have you used a comma after *however* and after *for example*?
- Have you used commas to separate items in a list?

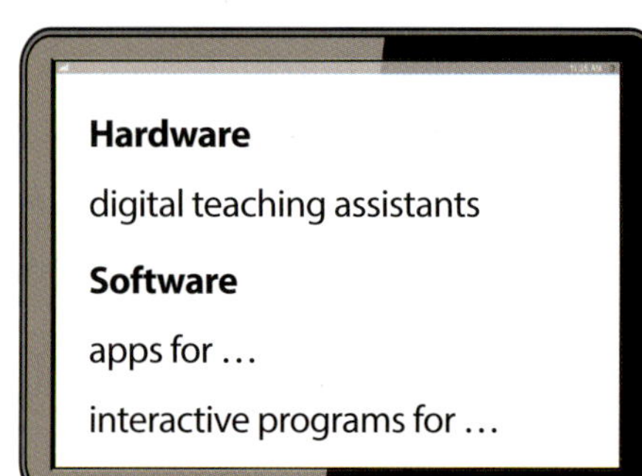

Technology at [*name of school*]

Introduce your report by saying how it is organised.

We have divided our report into three sections. The first section explains why we think technology is important in the classroom. The second section describes the technology we already have. The third section gives details of what we would like to have.

Number the sections.

1 Technology in the classroom

Studies suggest that most teachers think that technology can help students with reading, writing, listening and speaking. It is especially important for students who have difficulty with reading and writing, but it helps all of us to feel confident and to enjoy learning.

Give examples.

Teachers tell us that it can also save them a lot of time. For example, …

(preparing lessons, marking, keeping records of marks, …)

2 The situation at present

Start with the positive aspects.

Some of our classrooms have interactive whiteboards. A few have …

Link your arguments by using connectives such as *however*.

However, there are no classrooms that have …

3 The future

Show that you have done your research by referring to things you have read about.

In the future, AI will be used much more in teaching. For example, we have read about a digital teaching assistant, answering students' questions and helping them with their work. This saves the teacher a lot of time. We have also learned that it is possible to have language lessons personalised, so that they are based on the student's own situation (for example, their family and their interests).

5.8 Project challenge

Project 1: Technology that changed our lives

You are going to design a timeline to illustrate how technology has changed our lives.

1. Work in groups. Decide on the period you want to cover. The last 100 years? The last 50 years?
2. Divide the work among the students in your group.

   Let's take 20 years each. Sara, will you find out about the years 1920 to 1939? And Theo, will you look at 1940 to 1959? ...

3. How are you going to present your timeline? On a long piece of paper? On a poster? On a computer screen? Design your timeline.
4. You can illustrate your timeline with photos or drawings.

1923

Garrett Morgan invented the traffic signal

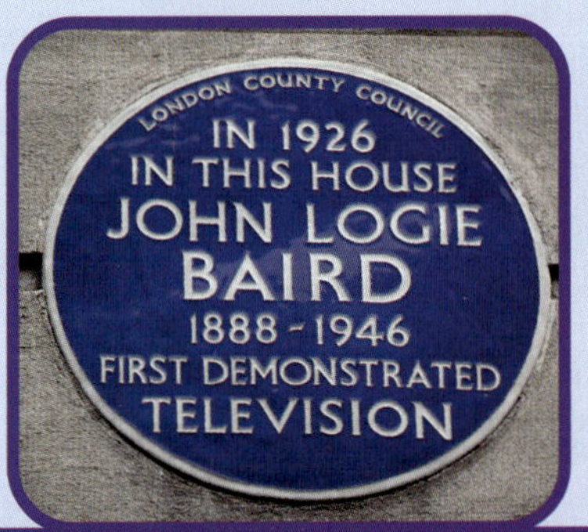

1926

John Logie Baird demonstrated television

5. Compare your timelines.
   - What did you learn from looking at the timelines created by other groups?

- What do you have to think about when creating a timeline?
- Would you change anything on your timeline, now that you have compared it with the timelines of other groups?

Project 2: A technology timeline for the future

You are going to make a technology timeline for the future.

1 Work in groups. You are going to invent a timeline for the future. Decide on the period you want to cover. The next 20 years? The next 50 years? The next 100 years?

2 Discuss what you think will be invented and what will change in that period: at home, at school, in the world around you.

- Ask questions to find out detailed information.
- Ask questions to find out exactly what someone means.
- Ask for reasons for a particular choice.
- Decide what should be included on the timeline.

A: ***I think that by about 2028, all new homes will be smart homes, controlled by the internet of things.***

B: ***What will they be like?***

A: ***The temperature and the lighting will be controlled automatically; your meals will be cooked for you …***

B: ***That sounds great! Yes, let's include that on the timeline!***

By 2028 …

All new homes will be smart homes, controlled by the internet of things.

By 2030 …

The majority of cars will be powered by hydrogen.

3 Design your timeline.

4 Present your timeline to other groups. Be prepared to answer questions about it.

5 Ask other groups questions about their timelines.

Will we control smart homes from our phones?

Why is hydrogen a clean fuel?

- When you were creating your timeline, what was easy and what was difficult?
- Now that you have answered questions on your timeline, would you change anything?

5.9 Non-fiction

***A Little History of Science* by William Bynum**

Professor William Bynum is a historian who writes about science and medicine. His book, *A Little History of Science*, begins: 'Science is special. It's the best way we have of finding out about the world and everything in it – and that includes us.'

The book tells the story of science from the earliest times to the present day.

1 **Read and listen to the extract below from Chapter 1, 'In the beginning'. What do you think William Bynum's aim was in writing this book?**

2 **William Bynum gives clues to help the reader understand some of the more difficult words he uses. Find these words in the text. Read the sentences (or parts of sentences) before and after them and try to work out their meaning.**

- a edible (line 8)
- b tally marks (line 31)
- c astronomy (line 47)
- d constellation (line 59)
- e astrology (line 64)
- f horoscope (line 70)

3 **Answer these questions.**

- a According to William Bynum, why are human beings interested in science?
- b Why is archaeology important in helping us to understand the history of early civilisations? Give an example.
- c How would you illustrate a 'tally' mark?
- d How did the Babylonians see the universe?
- e What impression do you get of the Babylonians?

4 **Work in groups. Discuss this question about the style of the extract.**

Is William Bynum's writing heavy, difficult and serious? Or is it light, quite easy to understand and engaging? Give examples to illustrate your opinion.

In the beginning, technology (which is about 'doing') was more important than science (which is about 'knowing'). You need to know what to do, and how to do it, before you can successfully grow your crops, make your clothes, or cook your food. You don't need to know *why* some berries are poisonous, or some plants edible, to learn how to avoid the one and grow the other. You don't have to have a reason why the sun rises each morning and sets each evening, for these things to happen, each and every day. But human beings are not only able to learn things about the world around them, they are also curious, and that curiosity lies at the heart of science.

We know more about the people of Babylon (in present-day Iraq) than we do about other ancient civilisations, for a simple reason: they wrote on clay tablets. Thousands of these tablets, written almost 6,000 years ago, have survived.

They tell us how the Babylonians viewed their world. They were extremely organised, keeping careful records of their harvests, stores, and state finances. The priests spent much of their time looking after the facts and figures of ancient life. They were also the main 'scientists', surveying land, measuring distances, viewing the sky, and developing techniques for counting.

We still use some of their discoveries today. Like us, they used tally marks to keep count; this is when you make four vertical marks and cross through these diagonally with a fifth, which you might have seen in cartoons of a prison cell, made by the prisoners keeping count of how many years they have been locked up. Far more importantly, it was the Babylonians who said there should be sixty seconds in a minute and sixty minutes in an hour, as well as 360 degrees in a circle and seven days in the week. It is funny to think that there is no real reason why sixty seconds make a minute, and seven days make a week. Other numbers would have worked just as well. But the Babylonian system got picked up elsewhere and it has stuck.

The Babylonians were good at astronomy – that is, examining the heavens. Over many years they began to recognise patterns in the positions of stars and planets in the sky at night. They believed that the earth was at the centre of things, and that there were powerful – magical – connections between us and the stars. As long as people believed that the earth was the centre of the universe, they didn't count it as a planet. They divided the night sky into twelve parts and gave each part a name associated with certain groups (or 'constellations') of stars. Through a heavenly game of Join-the-dots, the Babylonians saw pictures of objects and animals in some constellations, such as a set of scales and a scorpion. This was the first Zodiac, the basis of astrology, which is the study of the influence of the stars upon us. Astrology and astronomy were closely linked in ancient Babylon and for many centuries afterwards. Many people today know which sign of the Zodiac they were born under (I am Taurus, the bull) and read their horoscopes in newspapers and magazines for advice about their lives. But astrology is not part of modern science.

5 Read and listen to the second extract. It follows the one you have just read, but it moves on to a new topic. What is the topic?

The Babylonians were only one of several powerful groups in the ancient Middle East. We know most about the Egyptians, who settled along the River Nile as early as 3500 BCE. No civilisation before or since was so dependent on a single natural feature. The Egyptians relied on the Nile for their very existence, for every year as the mighty river flooded it brought rich silt to replenish the land around its banks, and so prepare it for the next year's crops. Egypt is very hot and dry, so a lot of things have survived for us to admire and learn from today, including many pictures, and a kind of pictorial writing, called hieroglyphics. After Egypt was conquered first by the Greeks and then by the Romans, the ability to read and write hieroglyphs disappeared, and so for almost 2,000 years the meaning of their writing was lost. Then, in 1798, a French soldier found a round tablet in a pile of old rubble in a little town near Rosetta, in the north of Egypt. It had a proclamation written in three languages: hieroglyphics, Greek, and an even older form of Egyptian writing called demotics. The Rosetta Stone came to London, where you can see it today in the British Museum. What a breakthrough! Scholars could read the Greek and therefore translate the hieroglyphs, decoding the mysterious Egyptian writing. Now we could really begin to learn about the ancient Egyptians' beliefs and practices.

[4] **to rely on:** to depend on

[6] **silt:** sand and soil that is carried by water and then settles, especially at a bend in the river

[6] **to replenish:** to fill or supply again

[13] **rubble:** broken stones or bricks from a building that has fallen down or been destroyed

[14] **proclamation:** an official public statement

[21] **to decode:** to discover the meaning of a message written in code

[24] **practices:** (in this text) customs

6 Work in pairs. Answer these questions.

- a What is the connection between the River Nile and the people who live near it?
- b What are hieroglyphs and why did people not know what they meant for almost 2,000 years?
- c The Rosetta Stone helped scholars to understand hieroglyphs. How?
- d The Rosetta Stone is in the British Museum in London. In your opinion, is that where it should be?

After writing about Babylon and Egypt, Professor Bynum goes on to write about science and technology in other early civilisations. One of them is China. He mentions the invention of paper, gunpowder and the compass.

7 Find out more about these inventions and write three short paragraphs about them, in the style of *A Little History of Science*.

Check your progress

General knowledge quiz

1 'Vlogging' is a combination of two words. What are the words, and what is 'vlogging'?

2 #

This symbol is used in music and it is sometimes used before numbers. What else is it used for?

3 In technology, what do these letters and numbers mean: AI, IoT, 3D?

4 It's a hard, shiny, white substance that has been used for many centuries for making cups and plates. What is it?

5 It was an empire that spanned the south-eastern part of Europe, the western part of Asia and the northern part of Africa. It lasted from the 13th to the 20th centuries. Its capital was Constantinople. What was it called?

6 In which sea is the Levantine Basin?

7 Where did the craze for drinking coffee begin?

8 If something is at the 'cutting edge' of technology, what does this mean?

9 Who found the Rosetta Stone, and where?

10 How many languages appear on the Rosetta Stone?

Vocabulary

Technology and social media

1 **Match the words to the definitions.**

data	emoji	selfie	spam

a a small digital image that expresses an idea or an emotion

b emails that you have not asked for, often containing adverts

c a photo that you take of yourself

d information in the form of text, numbers or symbols that can be used by or stored in a computer

2 **Match the words to make compound nouns and use them to complete the sentences.**

voice	mouse	cars	recognition
social	self-driving	mat	time
screen		media	

a Which ***social media*** platforms do you use?

b I got into trouble for not doing my homework, so Mum has limited my .... to an hour a day this week.

c My dad still uses a desktop computer, so I bought him a .... for it. I had a photo of our cat put on it.

d If you have difficulty typing on a keyboard, try using ....

e Do you think we will need to take a driving test in the future? After all, we'll be travelling around in ....

Use of English

1 **Read the information about the school sports day. Rewrite the sentences using the passive.**

A programme of events will be sent to parents.

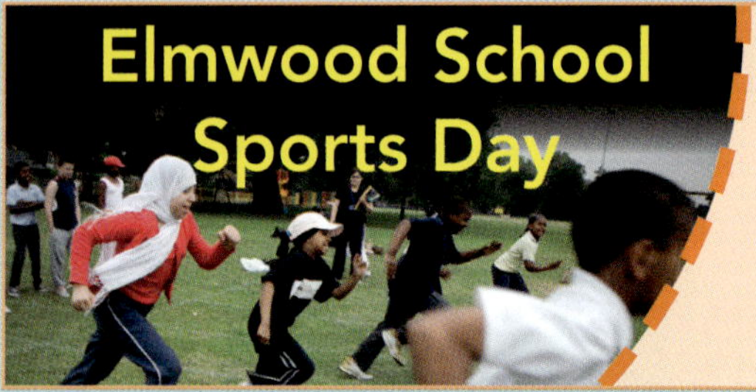

- We will send a programme of events to parents.
- We will give everyone a chance to take part.
- We will provide lunch and drinks.
- We will give the top three athletes prizes.
- A well-known local celebrity will award the prizes!

2 **The students at Elmwood School had some ideas for sports day. Use the words in the thought bubbles to write what they said.**

T-shirts poster
photos music
tent

make
print take
play put up

a 'We can have ***T-shirts made*** with "Elmwood School Sports Day" on the back.'

b 'We can have a .... with details of the day.'

c 'We can have .... by a professional photographer.'

d 'We can have .... by the school orchestra.'

e 'We can have a .... in the school field.'

3 **These people have just left school. Write a sentence explaining what each of them will be doing next year.**

a Sophie study medicine University of Amsterdam

Sophie will be studying medicine at the University of Amsterdam.

b Kishan work digital media company Seattle

c Tia teach secondary school Rome

d Samuel play football Toulouse Football Club

Summary checklist

I can

- ☐ describe the technology we will have in our homes in the future.
- ☐ take part in a discussion about social media and digital media.
- ☐ understand how archaeologists can use technology.
- ☐ make predictions of what life will be like in ten years' time.
- ☐ write a report on technology at school.
- ☐ read and understand extracts from a book about the history of science.

6 Rules and laws

In this unit you will...

- **listen to** and **discuss** opinions about school rules
- **read** a newspaper article about business practice and family life
- **talk** about rules at home
- **discuss** moral dilemmas
- **discuss** and **write** about rights and responsibilities
- **compare** two statements about the same incident
- **reply** to an email about rules at your school
- **record** a conversation about a moral dilemma for a podcast about social responsibility and citizenship
- **write** a witness statement
- **read** a true story of survival.

Getting started

"Why do we need rules?"

Watch this!

6.1 School rules

In this lesson you will...

- listen to and discuss opinions about school rules.

- **Is it possible to have a school without rules? Why / Why not?**

Listening

33

1 **Listen to an interview with students about their school. What impression do you get of the school?**

2 **Listen again. Answer the questions.**

a Give two examples of the school's rules.
The students have to … They mustn't …

b What are the students' opinions about the school?

c Can you tell what the interviewer's opinions are? Do you think she expected the students to answer as they did?

d What do you think about the rules at the school?

3 **Work in pairs. Describe the school using the words in the vocabulary box.**

strict	good behaviour	respect
break the rules	get into trouble	
get a detention	stay behind after school	

Remember

Use *have to* to talk about rules and laws:

They have to wear the correct school uniform.

Use *mustn't* to talk about what you are not allowed to do: *They mustn't talk in the corridors.*

Remember that *don't have to* is not the same as *mustn't*.

They don't have to have lunch in the school canteen. (They can have lunch there, but they can bring their own lunch, if they like.)

Use of English Verbs in the passive followed by the infinitive

To talk about rules, you can use the passive form of verbs such as *allow*, *encourage*, *expect*, and *suppose* followed by **to + infinitive**.

At lunch, we're expected ***to serve*** *the food and drinks for each other.*

We're not allowed ***to wear*** *earphones.*

Are you supposed ***to know*** *all the rules?*

4 **Complete the sentences about school rules around the world using the verbs in brackets.**

a In Japan, school children (*expect*) to help to clean and tidy the classrooms at the end of the day.

b Schools in France (*not / allow*) to serve tomato ketchup.

c At some primary schools in the UK, every student (*encourage*) to run a mile before lessons.

d In China, students (*expect*) to have a nap at midday.

5 **Complete the rules of the school you heard about in Exercise 1. Use the verbs in the Use of English box with the phrases from the list.**

answer teachers politely	interrupt when someone is speaking
chat to each other in class	look out of the window
talk to visitors	sit up straight in class
have a mobile out in class	talk in the corridors

They're expected to answer teachers politely.

They aren't allowed to …

Speaking

6 **Work in groups of three. Role-play the interview you heard or a similar interview about the rules at your school. One of you takes the role of the interviewer. The other two are the students. Start like this:**

Tell me, what's it like to be a student at this school? Are there a lot of rules?

Can you give me some examples?

7 **Work in groups. Discuss the questions.**

a Are rules important at school? Why?

b Which rules do you think are most helpful?

c What do you think leads to good behaviour? Is it only achieved by rules?

d Who should make the rules?

e Is it ever right to break the rules?

Speaking tip

These are some useful words and phrases you can use in a conversation.

- To start / introduce another idea: *Well …* *For one thing …* *Another rule is that …*
- To respond: *Right … OK … That's good … That's right … I see*

If you add 'Oh', you can add a tone of surprise: *Oh, right …* or *Oh, I see.*

6.2 Family life

In this lesson you will...

- read a newspaper article about a business strategy and family life
- discuss how and why a particular management practice can be useful in family life and in business.

Key words: Business studies

efficiency
employee
executive
management practice
process
productivity
schedule
set goals
system
workload

- **What are the best things about family life?**

Reading

1 **Read the newspaper article on the opposite page. How did a business idea help family life?**

2 **Work in pairs. Look at these words in context and discuss their meaning:**

- hectic
- household chores
- strategy
- knots
- pitch in
- resentment

3 **Answer the questions.**

a Why did the Swedish family decide they needed to make changes in their home life?

b Why did they choose a business method to help them make the changes?

c What kind of new rules did the family make?

d Why did they start having a family meeting once a week?

e Why do you think making schedules and setting goals were necessary?

f Has the process been a success? How do you know?

g Can you think of any disadvantages of the process?

Speaking

4 **Read the information about *kaizen*. Then discuss the questions.**

a Why do you think this method is used to improve productivity and efficiency?

b Does it need be a continuous process? Why?

c Is the process something that only managers and executives do, or does it involve other workers? Do you think this is an important part of the method? Why?

Language tip

The passive infinitive is formed with *to be* + a past participle.

*The house was in chaos, with piles of washing **to be done** and clothes **to be ironed**.*

Run your home like a business. This was the solution for a busy Swedish family.

Eva Jarlsdotter and her husband Mattias have three children. They live in Stockholm. Eva is a writer and businesswoman and Mattias is a doctor. At home, their life had become hectic, allowing little time for household chores. The house was in chaos, with piles of washing to be done and clothes to be ironed. Everyone was feeling stressed. They knew that something needed to change.

The family started to use a business strategy to sort out their chaotic homelife. Eva had seen how *kaizen* (the 'lean' method) produced big improvements in productivity and efficiency while working as an executive for a pharmaceutical company. Mattias had also witnessed how the system made things run more smoothly in hospitals.

Kaizen is a Japanese word for 'improvement'. It was first used as a process in business in Japan and then became part of management practices internationally. Kaizen was named the 'lean' method because it aimed to avoid waste and make work run smoothly by removing any problems. The idea is to continuously improve all work processes and to involve all employees in doing so.

Eva says that the family applied *kaizen* by first thinking about the process of running their home as a thread and tried to identify all the 'knots', the problems that were slowing things down.

First, they sorted their dirty clothes into four bags: one each for delicate fabrics, colours, white and black clothes. Every member of the family was expected to put their clothes in the correct bags, even Samuel, who was only two years old at the time.

According to the new house rules, when a laundry bag was full, whoever had filled it had to load it into the washing machine. Then they dried and ironed the clothes as soon as the load was finished.

The household chores are shared. Eva says, 'Our children – Vendela, now 16, Tuva, 14 and Samuel, ten – pitch in with everything from loading the dishwasher to doing the laundry. And there's no resentment over unfinished chores or unfair workloads.'

The family also decided that they needed a shared plan that was clear to everyone, so they wrote one and put it on their noticeboard. The plan is a two-week schedule that includes everything that they will be doing. On Sunday evenings, they have a 15-minute family meeting to discuss what is happening in the coming fortnight. They also set goals and decide how to resolve any problems as they arise.

According to Eva, by applying the 'lean' approach and making a few simple changes to their routines, they have made their home life happier and much more relaxed.

6.3 House rules

In this lesson you will...

- talk about rules at home
- report questions and statements.

- **Do families need rules? Why? What kind of things do you have rules about at home?**

Listening

34 1 **Listen to Alisha and Raheem comparing their families' rules. Are they similar or different?**

Vocabulary

2 **Work in pairs. What do these expressions mean? Explain them in your own words.**

a ban on (phones at the table)		a phone-free zone
screen time	make your bed	ask permission

3 **Listen to the conversation again. Then answer the questions.**

a What are the rules about the following?

- phones
- homework
- TV and video games
- doors
- lights and computers

b What three things do Alisha and Raheem have to ask permission for?

Speaking

4 **Work in pairs. Compare your family rules using the list in Exercise 2.**

Do you have rules about phones? We aren't allowed to …
What are the rules about homework? We're expected to … / We have to …

Listening

35 5 **Listen to Alisha and Raheem talking to their parents. What are they asking permission to do?**

Use of English Reported questions and statements

Direct speech	Reported speech
Questions	
• Use ***if / whether*** to report questions that can be answered with yes or no.	
Alisha: ***Can*** *I stay up late?*	*Alisha asked* ***if / whether*** *she* ***could*** *stay up late.*
Raheem: ***Are*** *we* ***doing*** *anything on Saturday?*	*Raheem asked* ***if / whether*** *they* ***were doing*** *anything on Saturday.*
• Notice the word order when you report questions beginning with a question word like *whose*, *what*, *where*.	
Raheem's dad: ***Whose*** *house* ***are*** *you* ***going*** *to on Saturday?*	*Raheem's dad asked Raheem* ***whose*** *house he* ***was going*** *to on Saturday.*
	(NOT ~~whose house was he going to~~)
Statements	
Say	
Alisha: *I* ***want*** *to watch the football match.*	*Alisha* ***said*** *she* ***wanted*** *to watch the football match.*
Tell	
• *Tell* must be followed by a personal object (*him*, *her*, etc.) or a name.	
Mum: You ***will*** *have to do your homework first.*	*Alisha's mum* ***told her*** *that she* ***would*** *have to do her homework first.*
Commands	
Mum: ***Clean*** *the kitchen afterwards!*	*Alisha's mum* ***told her to clean*** *the kitchen afterwards.*

6 **Choose the correct options to report the questions and statements.**

a Alisha to her mum: 'Can I make a pizza?'
Alisha ***said / asked*** if she ***can / could*** make a pizza.

b Raheem to his dad: 'We're going to play table tennis.'
Raheem ***said / told*** they ***are / were*** going to play table tennis.

c Raheem to his dad: 'Can I take the new balls to play with?'
Raheem ***said / asked*** if he ***can / could*** take the new balls to play with.

d Raheem's dad to Raheem: 'Bring them back.'
Raheem's dad ***said / told*** him to bring them back.

e Raheem's dad to Raheem: 'What time are you going?'
Raheem's dad ***asked / told*** him what time ***was he / he was*** going.

7 **Work in groups of three. Role-play asking a parent for permission to do one of the things below. One of you is the parent, one is the teenager and one will report the conversation.**

- Go to the beach on Sunday with a friend.
- Go to a friend's house to watch a film.
- Buy a new pair of trainers.

6.4 Doing the right thing

In this lesson you will...

- use *if / if only* in third conditionals
- discuss moral dilemmas.

- **What is a 'moral dilemma'?**

Reading

1 **Read these posts. How would you describe the attitude of the people who have written them?**

What would you have done?

One day after lessons, I was walking across the school football field on my way home when I saw some money on the ground. I picked it up but then I didn't know what to do with it. The school was closed so I couldn't go back there. In the end, I just left it where I'd found it. I thought that if someone had lost the money, they would have gone back to look for it. On the other hand, someone else might have found the money and kept it. What would you have done if you'd been in my position?

Brandon

I thought that a friend was having a problem with some classmates at school who were being unkind to her. I asked her about it and she said I was right, but she also asked me not to tell anyone because she thought it would make things worse. Not long after that, she started missing school. She said she wasn't feeling well. I thought, 'If only I had told a teacher about the problem with the other girls, the teacher would have sorted it out and my friend would be fine.' Should I have kept my friend's secret or should I have told someone straight away? What would you have done?

Rona

I had a drink and a sandwich at a café in town. When I had finished, I paid the bill and left. I was waiting at the bus stop when I realised I had only been charged for one item, not two. I remembered that the waitress who had served me was quite young and clearly new to the job. I could have gone back to the café, but I could see my bus coming and I didn't want to miss it. I got on the bus and went home, thinking I'd go back to the café when I was next in town. But I did worry that the girl might have got into trouble. What would you have done?

Bella

Use of English Third conditional

We use the **third conditional** to talk about imagined situations in the past – things that did not happen.

Clause 1: *if* + past perfect

Clause 2: *would have* / *could have* / *might have* + past participle

If someone ***had lost*** the money, they ***would have gone back*** to look for it. (But we don't know that happened – the situation is imaginary.)

You can reverse the order of the clauses:

If you had been in my position, *what would you have done?*

What would you have done ***if you'd been in my position***?

We use *if only* with the past perfect to talk about something you wish you had done.

Clause 1: *if only* + past perfect

Clause 2: *would have* / *could have* / *might have* + past participle

If only ***I had told*** *a teacher about the problem with the other girls, the teacher* ***would have sorted it out***.

2 **Match the sentence halves and write the complete sentences using the third conditional. Use *would have*, *could have* and *might have* as appropriate.**

If she (*look*) more carefully at the bill,

If we (*see*) someone drop the money in the field,

If only I (*persuade*) my friend to talk to her parents or a teacher,

If I (*go*) back to the café to explain the problem,

a she (not / get) so upset and missed school.

b the waitress (get) into trouble.

c she (notice) that there was a mistake.

d we (know) who to give it to.

Listening

36

3 **Listen to people talking about the situations in Exercise 1. What would they have done?**

a Brandon's dilemma

b Rona's dilemma

c Bella's dilemma

Speaking

4 **Work in pairs. Discuss what you would have done in the situations described in Exercise 1.**

Use *I would have ... / I wouldn't have ... / I might have ...*

6.5 Rights and responsibilities

Key words: Citizenship

- do jury service
- donate blood
- get married
- open a bank account
- vote
- work part-time / full-time

In this lesson you will...

- read about and discuss rights and responsibilities for teenagers.

- **At what age are you considered to be an adult?**

Reading

1 **Read the information about what you are allowed to do at certain ages in the UK. Does anything surprise you?**

In the UK ...

At 12 you can:
- buy a pet.

At 13 you can:
- open your own bank account.

At 14 you can:
- work part-time (with your school's permission).

At 16 you can:
- work full-time
- leave home and live independently (with your parents' permission)
- learn to drive if you are disabled and have permission from the government
- leave full-time education
- join the army.

At 17 you can:
- learn to drive.

At 18 you can:
- vote
- get married
- own a house
- give blood
- do jury service.

2 **Without looking at the text in Exercise 1, write seven collocations using the words in the two columns.**

work	a bank account
leave	full-time / part-time
get	home
join	the army
open	married
do	blood
give	jury service

You can do jury service when you are 18.

Speaking

3 **Work with a partner. What do you think about the age at which teenagers can buy a pet, open a bank account, etc. in the UK? Discuss each statement in the list in Exercise 1.**

A: ***What do you think about being able to buy a pet when you're 12?***

B: ***I don't agree with it. I think you're too young to be responsible for an animal at that age. What do you think?***

Writing

4 **Write a list, similar to the list in Exercise 1, giving information for teenagers in your country.**

- Find the information you need from the internet or other sources.
- Compare what you've found with what other students have found.
- Write your list.
- Compare and discuss the differences between your country and the UK.

6.6 What happened?

In this lesson you will...

- compare two accounts of the same incident and identify inconsistencies
- revise and extend the use of the past continuous.

- **A witness is someone who sees an event, such as an accident, happen. When is it useful for a witness to give a formal statement describing what happened?**

This photo was taken in London. In the UK, cars drive on the left-hand side of the road.

Speaking

1 **Look at the photo. Say what you think is going to happen. You can use the words in box below.**

parked car	accident
wing mirror	crash into
selfie stick	fall off
handlebars	

2 **Read two statements about what happened. Which do you think is the most reliable statement and why?**

Witness A

I was driving along the road behind the cyclist. There was a row of parked cars along the side of the road. I could see that the cyclist was holding the handlebars with his right hand and he had a phone on a selfie stick in his left hand. He was looking at the phone when someone in a silver Mercedes opened the car door. The cyclist didn't stop because he didn't see the person open the door. He hit the car door as it was opening and he fell off his bike. Fortunately, he wasn't going very fast. He wasn't wearing a helmet, but luckily he didn't hit his head and he wasn't badly hurt.

Witness B

I was standing on the pavement at the end of the street when I noticed a cyclist passing a row of parked cars. He had his arm out to show that he was going to turn left. He was wearing a blue T-shirt and blue jeans. I think he got too close to a silver van, which was behind a red car, when he was about to turn left. He caught the van's wing mirror and fell off his bike. It was just an accident as far as I could see. Fortunately, he was wearing a helmet so he wasn't badly hurt.

Use of English Past continuous

Remember that we use the past continuous to give background information and to describe a scene or a person.

*I **was driving** along the road behind the cyclist.*

*He **was wearing** a blue T-shirt and blue jeans.*

We use the past continuous and the past simple in the same sentence when one action interrupts another.

*He **was looking at** the phone when someone in a silver Mercedes **opened** the car door.*

Notice the use of *was going to* to show a past intention:

*He had his arm out to show that he **was going to** turn left.*

(He intended to turn left but he didn't do it.)

3 **Complete these statements by the driver of the car and the cyclist.**

- **Use the past continuous or the past simple of the verbs in brackets.**

  a I (cycle) along the road when a car door suddenly (open) in front of me.
  I was cycling along the road when a car door suddenly opened in front of me.

  b I (hold) the handlebars with my right hand when I (hit) the car door.

  c When the accident (happen), I (carry) my phone on a selfie stick.

  d The cyclist (crash) into the door as I (get) out of the car.

  e I (not / pay) attention when I (open) the door.

- **Use *going* to show past intention.**

  f I (get) my bag from the back of the car when a cyclist crashed into the door.
  I was going to get my bag from the back of the car when a cyclist crashed into the door.

  g We (exchange) names and addresses, but a police officer arrived and took statements from us and from two witnesses.

  h I (send) a video of my journey to college to my friends in Germany, but my phone got damaged in the accident.

Speaking

4 **Work in small groups. Discuss this question: Who was responsible for the accident, the driver or the cyclist?**

6.7 Improve your writing

In this lesson you will…

- reply to an email about rules at your school.

1 **Read the email from a student at an international school. Who is she writing to and why?**

Reply Forward

Dear Anisha,

I'm a student in Year 9 at Miraflores International School. I'm writing to you because we're doing a project about schools around the world and I thought it would be interesting to compare school rules from different countries. I would be very grateful if you could tell me about your school by answering some or all of the following questions.

To start with, what time are you expected to arrive at school in the morning? What happens if you're late? Do you have to report to the school office?

Is a school uniform compulsory at your school? What is it like? What happens if you're not wearing, for example, your tie or your jumper? Are there any rules about things like hairstyles or jewellery?

What rules do you have about behaviour in the classroom? Are you allowed to take phones to school? Are you allowed to have your phones on your desk during lessons? What are you supposed to do if you want to ask a question?

What about rules outside the classroom? For instance, are there any rules about moving around the school between lessons or at break time?

Finally, do you have any anti-bullying rules or guidelines at your school? For example, if you knew a student in your class was being bullied by others, what would you do? What are your views, overall, about the rules in your school?

I'm looking forward to hearing from you, and I'd appreciate any information you can send me.

Best wishes,

Isabel

2 **Answer the questions.**

- a How would you describe the tone of the email?
  - very formal
  - quite formal but friendly
  - very informal
- b Which sentence in the opening paragraph is particularly polite, and why?
- c How does Isabel make the closing sentence sound both friendly and polite?
- d Why do you think the email has several short paragraphs?

3 Read the reply from Anisha below. Then answer the questions.

- a Does Anisha answer all of Isabel's questions?
- b Which sentences does Anisha use to make her reply sound polite and helpful?
- c Does Anisha include any personal opinions or information? If so, what are they?
- d What impression do you get of Anisha and her attitude towards her school?
- e What is your impression of Anisha's school?

4 Using Anisha's email as a model, write your own reply to Isabel.

Remember to:

- start your email in a polite but friendly way
- answer all the questions in the order Isabel asked them
- give your own opinions at the end of the letter.

Reply Forward

Dear Isabel,

Thank you for your email. I think your project sounds very interesting, and I would be delighted to answer your questions about my school.

We are expected to arrive at school by 8.30 a.m., so I usually try to be there around 8.15 because I hate being late. If you are late, you have to report to the school secretary in the school office. Then you go straight to your tutor group. You have to say that you are sorry for being late and explain why.

Yes, we do have to wear a school uniform, but the school isn't too strict about things like not wearing your tie or jumper. We're not supposed to wear jewellery, but it's OK to wear, for example, simple earrings. We're not encouraged to have unusual hairstyles or hair colours!

When it comes to the classroom, we're expected to be polite and respectful to the teacher and to each other. We're not meant to interrupt when someone is speaking, make silly noises or try to make other students laugh. If we want to ask a question, we have to put up our hand.

Outside the classroom, we can move around and talk to each other quite freely, as long as we don't shout, push other students or disturb other classes.

In terms of anti-bullying policies, we are encouraged to report irresponsible or bullying behaviour to a staff member. It's never happened, but if I had seen someone being bullied, I would have talked to my tutor group teacher about it.

Overall, I think that our rules are quite reasonable because they help to make the school well-organised, without being too strict.

I hope my answers are helpful.

Best wishes,

Anisha

6.8 Project challenge

Project 1: Make a podcast

You are going to record a conversation about a moral dilemma for a podcast about social responsibility and citizenship.

1 Work in small groups. Read and discuss the following dilemma or, if you prefer, discuss a dilemma you or someone you know has had.

> A friend told me that a classmate had put some information about her on social media that was completely false. She was very upset. I reminded her that our school has a 'zero tolerance' policy on cyber-bullying and that she should report the incident to a member of staff. She said she didn't want to do that because she thought it would make things worse. She told me not to mention it to anyone. She wasn't at school the next day and did not return for the rest of the term, due to anxiety and depression.
>
> I thought that if only I had mentioned it to a teacher at school, we might have been able to help her. If someone tells you something in confidence, should you always keep their secret? What would you have done?

2 Discuss what you would have done in the situation. Include as many different ideas as possible.

3 Prepare to record your conversation.

- Decide who is going to start and what he / she will say.
- Make sure everyone in the group knows in what order they will speak.
- Respond to what other members of your group say.

It doesn't matter if you hesitate or make mistakes. You can correct what you or someone else said: *What I meant to say was … / Did you mean to say …?*

4 Record your conversation.

5 Play your conversation for the rest of the class to listen to. Ask them to say which ideas they agree or disagree with.

Speaking tip

I agree with you about …

I think you're right …

I see your point … / That's a good point …

I can see what you mean but …

- What did you find most interesting about the conversation you had and those you listened to?
- Did you change any of your own opinions when you listened to other students' views? Why?

Project 2: Write a statement

You are going to write the statement that the girl in the newspaper story below gave to the police.

TEENAGE GIRL SAVES FAMILY FROM FIRE

Teenage schoolgirl Chantale Adebayo saved her parents and her three-year-old sister from a fire which destroyed their home. Chantale woke up at around midnight and smelled smoke. She immediately woke her parents and carried her sister down the stairs and out of the house. She said that although the house was full of smoke, they were all able to escape unhurt.

1 Write a statement from Chantale Adebayo's point of view.
Remember the following:
- Tell the story in chronological order. In other words, describe the events in the order in which they occurred.
- Only give facts, not opinions.
- If you're not sure of something, don't say it.
- If you heard anybody say anything, report their words as accurately as possible.

2 When you have written your first draft, ask another student to read it and comment on it.

3 Write your final draft.

- What did you find most challenging about writing a statement?
- Did this task make you think differently about how you remember or report a past event? Why?

6.9 Non-fiction

In his book *Humankind,* Rutger Bregman finds examples from recent and historical events to disprove the idea that humans are essentially selfish. His evidence shows that, in fact, particularly in times of crisis and disaster, people tend to co-operate and work together to survive.

One of the examples is the story of six schoolboys from Tonga, a group of islands in the South Pacific Ocean, east of Australia. The boys planned an adventure. One night, they took a fishing boat from the harbour in Nuku'alofa, and set out to sea. Unfortunately, they all fell asleep and the boat drifted a long way from shore. They drifted for eight days without food or water before landing on a rocky, uninhabited island called Ata. The boys survived there for over a year before being found by an Australian sea captain, Peter Warner.

Rutger Bregman

1 **Read about *Humankind*. Then answer the questions.**

a What kind of book is it?

b What does it aim to do?

c Was the boys' 'adventure' a good idea? Why / Why not?

2 **Read and listen to the extract from Chapter 2 of *Humankind*.**

How did the boys find ways to do the following?

a get food

b have water to drink

c cook and keep warm

d keep themselves fit and strong

e be organised

f find solutions to disagreements

g keep themselves happy

3 Values **Work in small groups. Discuss the questions.**

a Why do you think the boys made rules?

b What do you think this real-life story tells you about human nature?

c What do you think happened when the boys eventually got back home to Tonga?

Chapter 2

'By the time we arrived,' Captain Warner wrote in his memoirs, 'the boys had set up a small commune with a food garden, hollowed-out tree trunks to store rainwater, a gymnasium with curious weights, a badminton court, chicken pens and a permanent fire, all from handiwork, an old knife blade and much determination.'

It was Stephen – later an engineer – who, after countless failed attempts, managed to produce a spark using two sticks. The boys tended their flame so it never went out, for more than a year.

The kids agreed to work in teams of two, drawing up a strict roster for garden, kitchen and guard duty. Sometimes they quarrelled, but whenever that happened they solved it by imposing a time-out. The squabblers would go to opposite ends of the island to cool their tempers, and, 'After four hours or so,' Mano later remembered, 'we'd bring them back together. Then we'd say "Okay, now apologise." That's how we stayed friends.'

Their days began and ended with song and prayer. Kolo fashioned a makeshift guitar from a piece of driftwood, half a coconut shell and six steel wires salvaged from their wrecked boat – an instrument Peter has kept all these years – and played it to help lift their spirits.

And their spirits needed lifting. All summer long it hardly rained, driving the boys frantic with thirst. They tried constructing a raft in order to leave the island, but it fell apart in the crashing surf. Then there was the storm that swept across the island and dropped a tree on their hut.

Worst of all, Stephen slipped one day, fell off a cliff and broke his leg. The other boys picked their way down after him and then helped him back up to the top. They set his leg using sticks and leaves. 'Don't worry,' Sione joked. We'll do your work, while you lie there like King Taufa'ahau Tupou* himself!'

The boys were finally rescued on Sunday 11 September 1966.

Physically, they were in peak condition. The local physician, Dr Posesi Fonua, later expressed astonishment at their muscled physiques and Stephen's perfectly healed leg.

** King Taufa'ahau Tupou is the king of Tonga*

1 **memoirs:** memories that are written down

2 **commune:** a group of people who live together and share work and resources

2 **hollowed-out:** with the middle taken out to create a space

7 **tend:** care for, look after, (*here*) keep the fire burning

9 **draw up:** make a plan in writing

9 **roster:** a list of names and the jobs each person has to do

10 **quarrel:** to have a disagreement

11 **squabblers:** people who have a disagreement over something

15 **fashion:** to make

16 **makeshift:** simple and not well-made but fulfilling a need

16 **driftwood:** wood that has been carried to the shore by the sea

17 **salvage:** save something from destruction

18 **lift (someone's) spirits:** to make (someone) feel happier

20 **frantic:** desperate

21 **fall apart:** break into pieces

24 **pick your way:** (*here*) to walk carefully over rocky ground

28 **in peak condition:** physically very healthy

Turn to the next page to find out what happened when the boys got home.

The mood when the boys returned to their families in Tonga was jubilant. Almost the entire island of Ha'afeva – population nine hundred – had turned out to welcome them home.

[…]

Peter [Captain Warner] returned to Sydney, resigned from his father's company and commissioned a new ship. Then he had the six boys brought over and granted them the thing that had started it all: an opportunity to see the world beyond Tonga. He hired Sione, Stephen, Kolo, David, Luke and Mano as the crew of his new fishing boat.

The name of the boat? The *Ata*.

[1] jubilant: very happy
[2] entire: all of
[3] turn out: to come to see something special
[6] commission: (here) to order a ship to be prepared for use
[7] grant: to give

Writing

4 **The boys have just returned to Tonga after being shipwrecked on the uninhabited island of Ata for more than a year. You are interviewing them for your newspaper. Describe their homecoming and include what they told you about their experiences.**

When the six lost boys from Tonga returned home, there were scenes of great joy and happiness. I was able to ask them about their experiences of surviving on a deserted island. They told me that …

5 Values **Work in groups. Discuss these questions.**

a What do you think the boys thought about their experiences at sea and on the island, once it was all over?

b What do you think you would have found hardest if you had been with them on the island?

c Do you think the story of the boys from Tonga is a good example of Rutger Bregman's theory about human nature? Why?

d Can you think of any examples from personal experience or recent world events that illustrate positive behaviour in difficult times?

e How did Captain Warner make the boys' dreams come true? Why do you think he did this?

Check your progress

General knowledge quiz

1 What are French school children not allowed to eat with their lunch?

2 Where is Stockholm?

3 Which language does the word *kaizen* come from and what does it mean?

4 In the UK, at what age can you open a bank account?

5 What does it mean if you work 'part-time'?

6 If you are asked to be part of a group of people who decide on a case in a court of law in the UK, you are going to do what?

7 What do you call a person who sees an event such as an accident and who gives a formal statement about what they saw?

8 On which form of transport would you find handlebars?

9 Why do cars and lorries have wing mirrors?

10 Someone who drives a car is a driver. What do you call someone who rides a bike?

Vocabulary

1 **Complete the text with the words from the list.**

behaviour bullying detention
respect rules strict trouble

Our school is quite ....[1]. There are a lot of ....[2] and if you don't follow them, you get into ....[3] and you sometimes get a ....[4], and have to stay behind after school. Good behaviour and ....[5] for other people are important. I think discipline is a good thing because it means there isn't much bad ....[6], such as interruptions in lessons and ....[7] outside lessons.

2 **Complete the sentences with a verb from the box in the correct form.**

ask follow give get
leave make own

a It only takes a few seconds to .... your bed, but I sometimes forget!

b I need to .... permission to leave school early today.

c If you had .... the rules, you wouldn't have got into trouble.

d How old do you have to be before you can .... blood?

e I don't want to .... home until I've finished my education.

f I'd like to .... a house or a flat by the time I'm 30.

g My sister .... married last week and we all went to the wedding.

Use of English

1 Complete the sentences with the correct passive form of the verbs in brackets.

- a We have a list for household chores and everyone (*expect*) to help out.
- b We (*not / allow*) to have our phones at the table. It's a phone-free zone.
- c At school, we (*encourage*) to learn to play a musical instrument, but it's not compulsory.
- d I (*suppose*) to learn a poem for homework this evening but so far, I've only learned two lines.

2 Report the following conversation.

Alina: Tell me about your school.
Carla: What do you want to know?
Alina: Are there a lot of rules?
Carla: We have a few, for example, we aren't allowed to use mobile phones in the classroom.
Alina: That's the same at my school.
Carla: We have to wear a uniform.
Alina: Oh, we don't, but we can't wear jeans and things like that.
Carla: I don't mind wearing a uniform because you don't have to think about what you're going to put on in the morning!

Alina asked Carla to tell her about her school.
Carla asked Alina what she wanted to know.

3 Match the two halves of the sentences, putting the verbs into the correct form for the third conditional.

If you had put your clothes in the washing basket, I would have washed them for you.

If you (*put*) your clothes in the washing basket
If we (*leave*) earlier
If you (*not / arrive*) late for class three times this week
If I (*not / write*) my essay so quickly
If they (*read*) the question more carefully.

- a they (*get*) the answer right.
- b we (*not / miss*) the school bus..
- c you (*not / get*) a detention.
- d I (*wash*) them for you.
- e I (*not / have*) made so many spelling mistakes.

Summary checklist

I can

- ☐ talk about rules at school and at home, and report what other people said.
- ☐ discuss moral dilemmas and say what I would have done in the same situation.
- ☐ discuss rights and responsibilities
- ☐ identify inconsistencies in witness statements.
- ☐ make a podcast about a moral dilemma.
- ☐ read a true story about how making their own rules helped shipwrecked teenagers to survive.

7 Competition

In this unit you will...

- **summarise** what people say about sports and activities, and the effect they have on them
- **describe** what happens in two sports and give your opinions about them
- **use** a radio interview as the basis of a discussion on competitive and non-competitive sport
- **give** a description of a non-sporting competition
- **describe** photos of the natural world
- **write** a 'for and against' essay about competitive sport
- **give** a presentation of the rules of a game
- **prepare** an entry for a photography competition
- **read** an extract from a book about how to succeed.

Getting started

“Are both co-operation and competition important in sport? Why?”

Watch this!

› 7.1 Team sports or individual sports?

In this lesson you will...

- summarise what people say about sports and activities, and the effect they have on them
- use the past perfect simple and the past perfect continuous.

- **How many team sports can you name? How many individual sports?**

Listening

38 1 **Listen to three students, Emir, Maya and Linh. Which sports and activities do they enjoy? Are they team sports or individual activities?**

Emir: taekwondo, …

2 **Listen again. Answer these questions.**

a How old is Emir?

b What do we know about Emir when he was 9 and when he was 12?

c How is Emir's life different now from when he first started at his new school?

d How do you know that Maya has become a better swimmer?

e Why does Maya think swimming is a good sport to do? (Think of the type of sport it is and of its benefits.)

f How do we know that Linh and her friends really enjoyed the training session?

g What does Linh's teacher say are the benefits of games like rugby?

Vocabulary

3 **Work with a partner. Choose from the words and phrases below to summarise what Emir, Maya, Linh and Linh's teacher say about the advantages of individual and team sports. Listen again if you need to.**

Nouns	Adjectives	Verbs and verb phrases
confidence	confident	to concentrate
strength	strong	to respect (others)
patience	patient	to work better with others, to get on better with other people
relaxation	relaxed	to build stronger relationships
self-esteem		to improve your communication skills
stress		

Use of English Past perfect simple and past perfect continuous

Past perfect simple

I'd done *taekwondo since I was quite young, but I gave it up when I was 9.*

In this sentence, **I'd done = I had done**. This is the **past perfect simple**.

We use the past perfect simple when we want to refer to a time before a past action: Emir gave up taekwondo when he was 9. Before that, he had done it since he was quite young.

Past perfect continuous

I'd just moved to a new school and ***I'd been having*** *a difficult time.*

In this sentence, **I'd been having = I had been having**. This is the **past perfect continuous**.

We use the past perfect continuous when we want to show that something was in progress up to a particular time in the past: Emir took up taekwondo again when he was 12. Before that, he had been having a difficult time.

38 **4 Complete sentences a to c using the past perfect simple. Complete sentences d and e using the past perfect continuous. Listen again if you need to.**

a Before she took lessons, Maya .... never .... about swimming technique.

b Linh saw a rugby match on TV. Before that, she .... of rugby but she .... a game.

c Before the training session, most of Linh's friends .... never .... a rugby ball.

d Maya .... about having lessons for some time when she saw an advert for swimming coaching.

e Linh and her friends .... only .... for an hour when the coach blew the whistle.

Language tip

You can use 'They say …' to talk about what people generally say or think.

'***They say*** *that taekwondo can help you not only to become physically stronger but also to improve your mental strength.*' (Emir)

Maya begins a sentence with '*They say …*' to talk about the effects of physical exercise. How does she continue?

Speaking

5 Discuss these questions.

- What are the benefits of sport for children and teenagers?
- Which are better for people of your age: team sports or individual sports?

Vocabulary tip

Emir uses these multi-word verbs when he's talking about taekwondo. Try to include them in your discussion.

to be into	to be very interested in
to join in (a game)	to take part in something that a group of people are doing
to take something up	to start doing something (like a sport)
to give something up	to stop doing something (like a sport)

7.2 Try this!

In this lesson you will...

- read about two sports
- describe what happens in each of the sports and give your opinions about them.

Key words: Physical education

competitive sports / non-competitive sports
contact sports / non-contact sports
(opposing) team
participant
player (an attacking player, a defender)
to attack
to defend
to score points / a goal

- **Which is the most enjoyable sport to watch? Why?**

Speaking

1 **Work with a partner. Before you read the text on the opposite page, look at the photos. Do you recognise either of these sports? What do you think happens in them?**

Reading

2 **Read the descriptions of the sports on the opposite page. What are the questions for these answers?**

a No, you can only use your feet, knees, chest and head.
b Rattan.
c It's twice the size of a badminton court.
d Between two and four players.
e It's different because it's a non-competitive sport.
f There are seven players in each team.
g Forty-five minutes.
h 'Kabaddi kabaddi'.
i You get one point for each person you touch.
j Tamil Nadu, about 4000 years ago.

3 **Think about it …**

a Which requires more skill, volleyball or sepak takraw?
b Why does the attacking player have to keep saying 'kabaddi'?

4 **Copy and complete the chart.**

	Sepak takraw	Kabaddi
Contact / non-contact sport?	*Non-contact*	
Competitive / non-competitive?	*Both*	
Teams, players		
Equipment		
Time limit?	*No. The first team to get 21 points wins.*	
Location	*Indoors (on a court) or outdoors*	

Speaking

5 Work in pairs. Use your chart and the words in the physical education key words box to tell each other about the sports featured in this lesson. Then say which one you would choose to do and say why.

This action-packed game is like volleyball, with one important difference: you can't use your hands to get the ball over the net. You use your feet, knees, chest and head to move the ball around. The ball is made of rattan, a thin type of cane that grows around larger trees in the rainforests of Africa, Malaysia and the Philippines, and is often woven to make furniture.

Sepak takraw is usually played on an indoor court that is twice the size of a badminton court, but it can be played outdoors too. It is a non-contact sport. There are two teams of two to four players. The first team to reach 21 points wins.

The origins of sepak takraw are found in Malaysia in the 15th century. Some versions of sepak takraw were not competitive: they were co-operative displays of skill designed to exercise the body and to improve flexibility. In Myanmar today, where sepak takraw is known as *chinlone*, teams play together, not in opposition to each other. It is a non-competitive sport in which the participants move gracefully, keeping the ball in the air for as long as possible.

This competitive contact sport is played between two teams of seven players each. A game lasts for 45 minutes, which includes a 5-minute break at half-time. **Kabaddi** can be played indoors or outdoors on a surface measuring 13 m × 10 m, separated into two halves by a white line. Points are scored as one player takes a deep breath and enters the opposing team's half chanting 'kabaddi kabaddi' and tries to touch as many members of the opposing team as possible without getting caught. The attacking player gets a point for each person they touch and must keep shouting 'kabaddi kabaddi'. The defenders either capture the player or prevent the player from getting back to their own side before taking another breath. Players need strength, speed and agility.

Kabaddi is an international sport that is said to have originated in Tamil Nadu, India about 4000 years ago.

7.3 To compete or not to compete?

In this lesson you will...

- listen to a radio interview and use it as the basis of a discussion on competitive and non-competitive sport
- use comparative and superlative adjectives and adverbs.

- **How many competitive and non-competitive sports and activities can you think of?**

Listening

39

1 Listen to this interview. How would you summarise the views of Matthew and Judy?

2 Answer the questions.

a According to Judy, why is competitive sport better than non-competitive sport?

b At one point in the interview, the presenter notices an inconsistency in what Judy says ('But you just said …'). What is the inconsistency?

c Can you tell what the presenter thinks of what Matthew and Judy say?

d Do both Matthew and Judy support their views with evidence? Give examples.

e Is either Matthew or Judy biased in what they say? (Do their personal opinions lead them to conclusions that are not based on fact?)

Vocabulary

3 Choose the correct meaning of the phrases in bold.

a For students **who are turned off by** competitive sport, non-competitive sport is more important.
  i who really enjoy ii who don't enjoy at all

b We don't want them **to be put off** because they can't jump as high.
  i to be made to dislike something ii to be told they are no good

c 'Non-competitive' sport **is all very well**, but does it prepare you for life?
  i OK in some situations ii good in all situations

d Competition **is a fact of life**.
  i is good for you ii exists and you have to accept it

e If you lose, you've got **to pick yourself up** and try again.
  i choose something different ii recover as quickly as you can

4 **Choose comparative or superlative forms to fill the gaps in these sentences with one or two words.**

a Non-competitive sport can make them feel .... (*good*) about themselves, ... (*relaxed*) and in fact .... (*sociable*).

b We don't want them to be put off because they can't compete with those who jump the .... (*high*), or run the .... (*fast*).

c If you lose, you've got to pick yourself up and try again. That's the .... (*valuable*) lesson you can learn in life.

d You might not be able to run as .... (*fast*) as the others, but perhaps you're .... (*good*) at longer distances than they are. You may be able to run .... (*far*) than the others.

e We should be much .... (*concerned*) than we are that children are .... (*satisfied*) with their lives than they were ten years ago.

Use of English Comparatives and superlatives

Look at the list of adjectives and adverbs. Which ones do the speakers in the interview use, and what are they referring to when they use them?

Adjectives

high	higher	highest
happy	happier	happiest
patient	more patient	most patient
rewarding	more rewarding	most rewarding
good	better	best
bad	worse	worst
far	farther / further	farthest / furthest

Adverbs

Short adverbs have the same form as adjectives:

fast	faster	the fastest
high	higher	the highest

Other adverbs follow this pattern:

carefully	more carefully	the most carefully

Be careful with *well* and *badly*:

well	*better*	*the best*
badly	*worse*	*the worst*

Use *as … as* to say that things are equal or not equal.

You might not be able to run ***as fast as*** the others.

Less … (than) is similar to *not as … (as)*.

That student was ***less*** *stressed during the exam period because she was doing yoga.*

The superlative form of *less* is *least*.

What is the ***least*** *stressful job you can think of?*

Speaking

5 **Organise a class discussion on competitive and non-competitive sports.**

- Divide the class into four groups. Two people from each group are going to present the views of their group.
- Help the speakers prepare what they are going to say. Try to include some of the phrases from Exercises 3 and 4.
- Link your ideas using simple connectives such as *and*, *but*, and *so*. Use *However,* to introduce a contrasting point.
- If you think that something isn't quite clear, you can say 'What I mean is …' and explain it in a different way.
- When the speakers have presented their views, the whole class can ask questions. To make it clear what you are referring to, start your question with 'You said that … .'

7.4 Two competitions

In this lesson you will...

- listen to descriptions of two non-sporting competitions and give a description of a similar competition of your choice
- use the past perfect simple, active and passive.

- **Apart from sports competitions, what other sorts of competition are there?**

Vocabulary

40

1 **Listen to the words for events and people who take part in them. Repeat the words, making sure you put the stress on the correct part of the word.**

Event	Person
competition	competitor
contest	contestant
challenge	challenger
championship	champion

Stages of a competition

(qualifying) round	quarter-final
semi-final	final
(to compete for, to win) a title	

Listening

41

2 **Listen to these two news reports of competitions. Have both competitions already finished?**

3 **Answer these questions.**

a What is *Junior Bake Off*?

b What are the stages of *Junior Bake Off*? (Use the words in the Vocabulary box to help you describe them.)

c In *Junior Bake Off*, what is a 'showstopper'?

d What is Zak's 'showstopper'?

e At what time of year did the World Women's Chess Championship take place?

f How many times has Ju Wenjun won the championship?

g 'At six games all, the result was decided by a tie-break.' What do you think a 'tie-break' is? Do other games have something similar? (Think of tennis and football, for example.)

h How has playing chess influenced Ju Wenjun?

Ju Wenjun

Use of English Past perfect simple, active and passive

Look at this sentence:

Thousands of young people ***had applied*** *and he* ***had been chosen****!*

(active: *had applied*; passive: *had been chosen*)

The subject of the verb is 'Thousands of young people'.

We do not know the subject of the verb.

What happens when you report a statement that contains a verb in the present perfect (or the past) passive?

'I ***have been helped*** *to prepare for the championship by my personal coach Ni Hua and by the head coach of China's national team, Ye Jiangchuan.'*

Ju Wenjun ***said*** *she* ***had been helped*** *to prepare …*

4 **Choose the past perfect simple active or passive to complete these sentences. You can listen again to check your answers.**

a It was one of the best moments of his life when 13-year-old Zak Travess found out that he .... (*gave*) the chance to appear on *Junior Bake Off*.

b When we met, she .... (*just / award*) the title of Women's World Chess Champion, the greatest honour in women's chess, for the third time.

c Her opponent .... (*show*) great determination and skill.

d The first six games .... (*play*) in Shanghai, before the players flew to Vladivostok for the remaining six.

Remember
Ordinal numbers

… for the ***third*** *time*

1st	first
2nd	second
3rd	third
4th	fourth

Writing and speaking

42

5 **Think of a competition in your country. Write a short description of it, without naming it. Read out your description to the class. Can they guess what the competition is? Try to keep them guessing as long as possible! You can listen to an example to help you.**

7.5 The art of photography

In this lesson you will...

- learn about a 'Young Photographers' competition
- describe photos of the natural world.

Key words: Photography

background
flash
out of focus
silhouette
tripod
zoom lens

- **People disagree about whether photography is an art, like painting. What do you think?**

Reading

1 **This is how the RSPCA Young Photographer Awards are introduced on the 'Young RSPCA' website. Is it a good introduction? Give reasons for your answer.**

The aim of our RSPCA Young Photographer Awards is to encourage an interest in photography and an appreciation and understanding of all the amazing animals around us. [The competition] is open to anyone aged 18 or under and all we want is for you to enjoy the process and get creative.

RSPCA: The Royal Society for the Prevention of Cruelty to Animals is an animal charity in Britain that aims to make sure animals are looked after and treated well.

2 **Use the words in the photography key words box to complete the tips on taking photos for the competition.**

Tips from the experts

A .... is useful if you can't get close to the animal you want to photograph.

Use a .... if you need to hold the camera steady for a long time.

Whether you're indoors or outdoors, try taking photos with and without a ....

Try making a .... of an animal by taking your photo with the light behind it.

A .... that is .... can help to draw the attention to the subject of the photo.

3 **Work in groups. Answer these questions.**

- a One of the rules of the competition reads: 'Please give each photo a title and write a description.' Why do you think the judges ask for this?
- b What advice would you give someone who wants to photograph birds in flight?
- c Which of the photos on these pages do you like best? Give your reasons.

Writing

4 **Work individually or in pairs. Write your answers to these questions. (You can discuss your answers with a partner if you like.)**

- a What title would you choose for each of the photos on these pages?
- b How would you describe each of the photos?

Speaking

5 **Compare what you have written for Exercise 4 with what other members of the class have written.**

7.6 A towering achievement

In this lesson you will...

- listen to a description of a competition and then give your own description
- use connectives such as *so that*, *however* and *finally*.

- **Are some competitions dangerous? Give examples to support your answer.**

Listening

43

1 Listen to this description of a competition. Then write a short caption for the photo.

2 Complete the chart to give information about this competition.

When?	Every two years, in the month of …………
Where?	City: Tarragona; region: Catalonia; country: …………
What happens?	Teams of people called *castellers* build human …………
Why?	It's a symbol of …………
Music?	Yes. Pipes and …………

Use of English Connectives

Conjunctions are a type of **connective**. They are used to connect parts of a sentence.

The heavier members of a team form a circle, ***so that*** *a strong base is formed.*

Examples: *and, but, so, because, when, before, after, as soon as, although, until, both … and, not only … but also …*

Connectives can also be used to connect ideas.

The smallest and lightest goes last and waves to the crowd in order to show that the building of the tower is complete. ***However,*** *that is not the end.*

And they can be used as 'signposts' in a text.

First, *the heavier members of a team form a circle.* ***Then,*** *…*

Examples: *Finally, In conclusion, On the one hand, … On the other hand, …*

Use a comma after connectives of this kind.

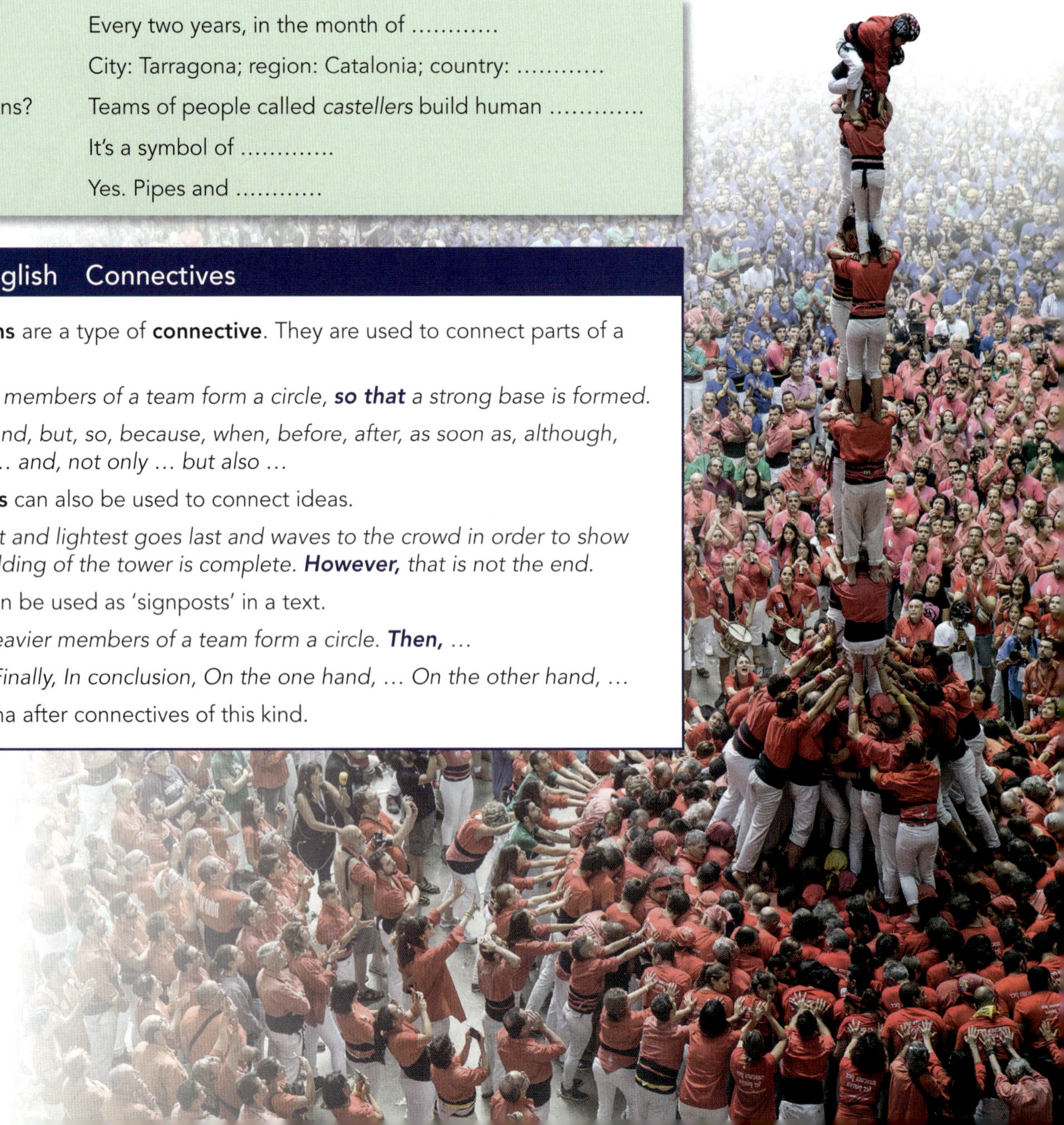

3 **Choose from the connectives in the box to complete these sentences. Then listen again and check.**

As	because	in order to	provided that
until	As soon as	not only … but also	

a You might say, 'You're building castles in the air', ………… something is unlikely to happen.

b ………… the first circle is formed, the more athletic members of the team climb onto their shoulders.

c Constructing the towers requires ………… strength of body ………… strength of mind.

d They continue, one level at a time, ………… the final level is complete.

e ………… the tower is being built, different tunes are played for the different levels.

f The smallest and lightest goes last and waves to the crowd ………… show that the building of the tower is complete.

g The tower is only a success ………… everyone comes down safely.

Speaking

4 **Work in pairs. Student A has just been to the human tower competition in Tarragona. Use the notes you made in Exercise 2 and your answers to Exercise 3 to describe it. Student B asks questions to make sure all the detail is included.**

A: *I saw the most amazing competition in Tarragona.*
B: *What was it?*

Listening

44

5 **Now listen to a description of another competition. Write a short caption for the photo.**

Speaking

6 **Work with a partner. Listen again and make notes. Then work together to describe the Chonburi buffalo race.**

7 **Work in groups. Discuss the two competitions.**

- Would you enjoy seeing them?
- Are they safe?
- What do you think about using animals in competitions such as the buffalo race?

7.7 Improve your writing

In this lesson you will...

- write a 'for and against' essay about competitive sport.

1 **Work in groups. First, discuss this question:**

If you were writing a 'for and against' essay about horse racing, what would your arguments in favour of ('for') it be? What would your arguments 'against' it be?

2 **Read the model essay on horse racing on the opposite page and answer these questions.**

- Does it use some of the arguments you thought of in Exercise 1?
- Can you tell whether the writer is for or against horse racing? Give reasons for your answer.

3 **In your groups, write a draft of the conclusion for the essay on horse racing.**

4 **Working individually, not in groups, you are now going to write an essay on competitive sport. Use the plan of the essay on horse racing and decide what you would put in the introduction, the second paragraph and the third paragraph.**

5 **Write a plan for the introduction and the second and third paragraphs.**

6 **Write a first draft of these three paragraphs. Use connectives to link clauses within sentences and to link your ideas. To help you use them, find these connectives in the essay on horse racing.**

because	such as	not only … but also …	Although
First, … Second, … Finally, …		However, …	In addition, …

7 **Write a draft. Check it and write your final version.**

8 **Read your final version to the class. The class can respond with questions and constructive comments.**

Introduction: introduce the topic and make clear what the 'for and against' issue is.

State the arguments 'for'. Support the arguments with facts and examples.

State the arguments 'against'. Support the arguments with facts and examples.

Conclusion

Should horse racing be banned?

On the one hand, …

On the other hand, …

Horse racing

Horse racing is one of the oldest competitive sports. People all over the world have enjoyed it for centuries. However, people are now asking questions about whether it should continue, because they say it is a cruel sport.

In the UK, horse racing is the second-biggest spectator sport after football. There are at least three good reasons for supporting horse racing. First, it brings money in and creates jobs. The total economic contribution of horse racing to the UK economy, for example, is about £3.5 billion, together with over 85,000 jobs. Second, race meetings bring people together, young and old, to enjoy a good day out. What is more exciting than to see a beautiful horse run well and win a race? Finally, children and teenagers who take part in competitions learn valuable lessons for life, such as determination and resilience, and, of course, how to deal with disappointment when they lose.

The main argument of people who are against horse racing is that it is a dangerous sport, not only for the horses but also for the riders. In the first four weeks of this year's race season, for example, five horses died at Santa Anita Park, a race track in California. Racehorses die most often from breaking a leg. For a human being, a broken leg is easily mended, but not for horses. Although it's a dangerous sport for horses, it's also dangerous for their riders. Studies have found riding to be more dangerous than skiing, car racing or football. In addition, racehorses are not always treated well and are not given enough time to rest between races. There are rules about using the whip, but people say that it is cruel to use the whip on a horse. Is it not enough to enjoy the company of horses without using them to compete? You get out in the fresh air, you make new friends and you learn how to look after animals and to respect them.

7.8 Project challenge

Project 1: A presentation of the rules of a game

You are going to do a presentation of the rules of a game.

1 Read through steps 2 to 4 and decide whether you want to work in pairs (Student A and Student B) or groups (Group A and Group B).

I think we should work in pairs because we'll get more variety that way.
I think it would be easier to work in groups because …

2 Student A / Group A: You want to introduce the game of **Ultimate Frisbee** to your school. Look up the rules and write a simple explanation of them. You can present them on slides or on a poster. You are also going to answer questions about the game.

Student B / Group B: **Boccia** (pronounced _Botch_-*a*) is a Paralympic sport. You have been to see a game and you're going to give a simple presentation of the rules, on slides or on a poster. You are also going to answer questions about it. Look up the rules and make notes about them.

3 Student A / Group A gives their presentation. Student B / Group B asks questions to make sure they understand the rules.

4 Student B / Group B gives their presentation. Student A / Group A asks questions to make sure they understand the rules.

- What were the advantages of working in pairs / groups?
- Could you now explain the rules of these two games to someone else?

Project 2: Enter a photography competition

You are going to enter a photography competition.

In Lesson 7.5, you read about the RSPCA Young Photographer Awards. You are going to enter a similar competition for photos of the natural world (which can include animals).

The photo must be taken with a camera or a mobile phone. You are not allowed to change the image by using a computer program.

1. Work individually or in pairs. Answer these questions.
   - Are you going to use a photo you already have, or are you going to take one specially for the competition?
   - Is your photo going to be in colour or black and white?
   - Is your photo going to be realistic or abstract?
2. The rules say that you have to give your photo a title and send a 'supporting statement' with your photo of up to 100 words. This statement will tell the judges why you took this photo and why you chose to send it. Write a draft title and statement.

   Look at Mei's photo and statement as an example.

> There is a plum tree growing on a wall near my house. I had never noticed it until one morning, when I was on my way to school it caught my eye and I had to take a photo of it. There had been snow during the night and some of it had stayed on the tree. I wanted to show both the beauty of the flowers and the strength of the branches with the snow on them. It reminds me of a painting on a vase.
>
> Mei, Beijing, China

3. Show what you have written to another student or another pair of students. Ask them for their comments.
4. Write a final version of your entry.
5. Present your photo to the class with its title and read out your statement.

- How did you choose a photo, or a scene to photograph?
- Why do you think the judges ask for a 'supporting statement'?

7.9 Non-fiction

***The Playbook* by Kwame Alexander**

Kwame Alexander is a poet, educator and bestselling author who regularly visits schools and speaks at conferences. The subtitle of *The Playbook* is: '52 Rules to Aim, Shoot and Score in This Game Called Life'. The extract is from the first chapter of the book.

45

1 **Read and listen to the extract. The first and last paragraph enclose the story of Wilma Rudolph – like a frame around a painting. Why do you think Kwame Alexander chose to frame the story in this way?**

2 **Work with a partner. Answer these questions.**

a What do we learn about the following?
- Wilma's family
- her experience of the segregation of black and white people
- her character as a child and as a teenager
- her achievements as a young adult
- the influence she had.

b Why do you think the young Kwame Alexander chose to write about Wilma Rudolph for his book report?

c According to Kwame Alexander, why is Wilma Rudolph a good role model?

d How is the story of Wilma Rudolph organised? Does it start from the present and go backwards in time, or does it start from her childhood and move forward in time towards the present?

3 **Find examples of:**
- time phrases which help the reader to understand what happened at various stages in Wilma Rudolph's life
- words that give a clue to Wilma's character.

4 **Work in groups. Discuss this question:**

What part did competition play in Wilma Rudolph's life?

[1] eighth grade: aged 13–14
[6] grab: to take hold of something suddenly
[6] slim: thin
[13] four and a half pounds: 2 kilos
[16] get this: make sure you pay special attention to this
[19] brace: a metal support
[20] Greyhound: an intercity bus company in the US
[22] therapy: treatment that does not involve a surgical operation
[24] segregation: the policy of keeping people of different races separate
[25] the Deep South: the states of Alabama, Georgia, Louisiana, Mississippi and South Carolina in the southern part of the US
[39] sheer: very strong
[39] willpower: the ability to control your thoughts and behaviour in order to achieve something
[50] gifted: naturally talented
[56] recruit: to get someone to join an organisation
[74] dash: (*American English*) a short race
[76] game changer: something that has big consequences
[80] induct: to officially accept someone into a group

Grit (*noun*): courage and resolve; strength of character.

In eighth grade, I had to do a book report, and I waited, as usual, until the very last minute. My house was pretty much a library, so I grabbed the first slim volume I saw off the shelf in our family room. It was a book about Wilma Rudolph, an Olympic track champion. It took me about an hour to read the book. Her story was remarkable. What I found out about her life changed mine.

When she was born, Wilma Rudolph weighed only four and a half pounds, and she spent the first eleven years of her childhood fighting illnesses such as scarlet fever, whooping cough, double pneumonia, and, get this, polio. Polio causes paralysis and has no cure. So, left with only one working leg, Wilma was fitted with a metal leg brace at around age five.

Every week, she and her mom took a Greyhound bus from their small town to Nashville, Tennessee, for her physical therapy, so that she could learn to walk with her brace. During these trips, Wilma witnessed and experienced the segregation of the Deep South – they always had to ride in the back of the bus, and they couldn't eat in most restaurants. Witnessing racial divides and experiencing her own disability gave Wilma grit and determination that would help her overcome some pretty huge challenges.

Often, Wilma would try to remove her leg brace so she could play like her friends and siblings. By age eleven, she finally kicked off that leg brace permanently and began practising to walk, run and play ball. It was painful and hard, but she was determined. Her brothers set up a basketball hoop in their yard, where she played every chance she got. After years and years of hard work and sheer willpower, she could not only walk well, but she could run faster than most kids. She became a star basketball player at her school, where Coach C. C. Gray gave her the nickname "Skeeter" because she was so fast. Imagine that: a girl who walked in special shoes with a leg brace for years was now given a nickname because of her speed.

Wilma became an all-state basketball player, setting the state record of forty-nine points in a single game. She was gifted, so gifted that word soon reached Ed Temple, track coach at Tennessee State University, who recruited her to start training with his team. Surprisingly, she qualified for the 1956 Olympic Games in Melbourne Australia, where she became the youngest member of the U.S. track team at just sixteen years old. She flew home with a bronze medal.

After high school, Wilma went to Tennessee State, where she studied education and trained for the next Olympic Games. Within four years, she was back at the Olympics, this time in Rome, Italy, where she set world records in the 100-metre dash, 200-metre dash, and the 100-metre relay. The Olympics were a huge success and a game changer for Wilma, as she became the first American woman to win three gold medals in a single Olympics. She was soon known as the world's fastest woman.

She was later inducted into the U.S. Olympic Hall of Fame and founded the Wilma Rudolph Foundation to help inspire and encourage amateur athletics. Not bad for a girl whose doctors said she would always have trouble walking.

When I presented my book report to the class, I ended by saying that we all face challenges and defeats in our life, but if you are self-determined and committed to putting in the work, you can bounce back like Wilma Rudolph did. I got an A+ on the report, but more important, I realised that if she could overcome a paralyzed leg and become a track star, then I could work hard and excel in whatever sport I chose – and perhaps, in life.

At school, Kwame Alexander wanted to be a top basketball player or footballer, but he wasn't as talented as his friends. His mother suggested tennis, which seemed really 'uncool' to him. However, she took him to the tennis courts for some practice, and eventually he not only made it on to the school tennis team but also won a district double tournament with his teammate Rob.

5 Values Work in groups. Read the quotes and discuss what each one means to you.

In *The Playbook*, Kwame Alexander quotes famous people 'who have overcome challenges to achieve amazing things.' Here are some of them.

> **Sport teaches you character, it teaches you to play by the rules, it teaches you to know what it feels like to win and lose – it teaches you about life.**
>
> *Billie Jean King, Hall of Fame thirty-nine-time Grand Slam tennis champion, founder of the Women's Tennis Association*

> **I have missed more than 9,000 shots in my career. I have lost almost 300 games. On 26 occasions I have been entrusted to take the game-winning shot and missed. And I have failed over and over and over again in my life. And that is why I succeed.**
>
> *Michael Jordan, six-time NBA (National Basketball Association) champion with the Chicago Bulls, five-times Most Valuable Player.*

> **Winning is great, sure, but if you are really going to do something in life, the secret is learning how to lose. Nobody goes undefeated all the time. If you can pick up after a crushing defeat and go on to win again, you are going to be a champion some day.**
>
> *Wilma Rudolph, three-times Olympic gold medallist, track and field*

> **No matter what accomplishments you make, somebody helped you.**
>
> *Althea Gibson, eleven-time Grand Slam tennis champion*

> **Surround yourself only with people who are going to lift you higher.**
>
> *Oprah Winfrey, TV producer, actor, author and talk-show host*

> **There is no magic to achievement. It's really about hard work, choices and persistence.**
>
> *Michelle Obama, lawyer, author and former First Lady of the USA*

6 Choose the quote that means most to you and write a paragraph to explain your choice, giving examples if you can.

Check your progress

General knowledge quiz

1 What is sepak takraw and where did it originate?

2 What do you call the interval between the two halves of a game?

3 What is the name of the sport that originated in Tamil Nadu, India about 4000 years ago?

4 In a competition, what do you call the stage between the quarter-final and the final?

5 Racket, ball, net, '15–love', set, singles, doubles, tie-break: What is the sport?

6 You play this game on a board of black and white squares with 16 pieces, including a king and a queen. What is the game?

7 What does the A stand for in the letters RSPCA – the Royal Society for the Prevention of Cruelty to …?

8 What do you call the kind of camera lens that lets you get closer and closer to an object?

9 Where is Tarragona and what is its connection with 'castles in the air'?

10 Where would you go to see a buffalo race that takes place every year and is part of a three-day festival: Thailand, Trinidad or Tunisia?

Vocabulary

1 **Complete the nouns that come from the following adjectives.**

	Adjective	Noun
a	successful	succ *e s s*
b	confident	confid _ _ _ _
c	strong	streng _ _
d	patient	pati _ _ _ _
e	relaxed	relax _ _ _ _ _

2 **Complete the second sentence so that it means the same as the first. Include a word from the list in Exercise 1.**

a You should feel very calm after doing yoga.
You'll feel very ………… after doing yoga.

b If you want to get to the top, you'll have to work hard.
If you want to achieve …………, you'll have to work hard.

c Taking the perfect photo takes time.
You'll need to be ………… if you want to take the perfect photo.

d You'll gradually become a little bit more sure of yourself.
You'll gradually build up your …………

e Even lifting light weights can increase your physical power.
Even lifting light weights can improve your …………

Use of English

1 Use the past perfect continuous to complete these sentences.

a I ***'d been trying*** (*try*) to solve a maths problem for half an hour. But it was really quite simple!

b We ……… (*live*) there for six months before we met her.

c How long ……… she ……… (*wait*) before she was able to join in the game?

d He ……… (*not / feel*) well for about a week, so he didn't play.

2 Complete the second sentence so that it means the same as the first.

a My sister's stronger than me.
I'm ***not as strong*** as my sister.

b You're better at the high jump than me.
I'm ……… as you.

c I'm more patient than you.
You're ……… than me.

d You're more confident than me.
I ……… as you.

3 Complete the sentences using superlatives.

a Of all the matches, this is the ***most important*** (*important*) match of the season.

b Which is the ……… (*difficult*) event of all in the competition?

c Who is the ……… (*fast*) runner in your school?

d We lost. It was the ……… (*bad*) match we've ever played!

4 Complete the biography of the dancer Anna Hayden with these connectives.

However	in order to	As
~~although~~	provided that	so

Her contract with the Bolshoi Ballet was for two years. She enjoyed her time in Moscow and achieved great success, ***although*** she missed her friends and family at home. She told the director that she was thinking of going home, ………… give him enough time to find a replacement. …………, he didn't want her to leave, ………… he persuaded her to stay, raising her salary. She agreed, ………… she could return home more frequently. ………… he was very keen for her to stay, the director said that could be arranged, and gave her a new contract.

Summary checklist

I can

- ☐ summarise what people say about sports and activities, and the effect they have on them.
- ☐ discuss competitive and non-competitive sport.
- ☐ describe photos of the natural world.
- ☐ write a 'for and against' essay about competitive sport.
- ☐ give a presentation about the rules of a game.
- ☐ prepare an entry for a photography competition.

8 The environment

In this unit you will...

- **learn** and **use** collocations for describing weather conditions
- **read** about the causes and effects of global warming
- **understand** and **express** opinions about global environmental issues
- **listen to** suggestions for reducing waste
- **discuss** the advantages and disadvantages of urban farming
- **understand** and **discuss** ideas about making cities sustainable for the future
- **write** a report about extreme weather conditions
- **present** plans for redeveloping an area of your city
- **read** and **analyse** two poems about the Earth and nature.

Getting started

"What kind of harm to the environment do you think is most dangerous for the planet?"

Watch this!

8.1 Let's talk about the weather

In this lesson you will...

- learn and use collocations for describing weather conditions
- use comparative and superlative adverbs of frequency.

- **What are the perfect weather conditions for each of the following: going to the beach, skiing in the mountains, playing in a football match, staying at home with your family?**

Vocabulary

1 **Match the weather forecast extracts to these symbols.**

a 
b 
c 
d 
e 
f 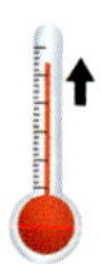
g 
h
i 
j 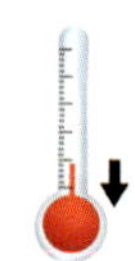

1. It'll be wet tomorrow. There'll be thunderstorms and heavy rain.
2. It will be windy all day but with strong winds in the late afternoon.
3. Tomorrow morning we'll see a heavy frost in most places.
4. Temperatures will fall rapidly this evening.
5. Temperatures will rise to 40 °C during the course of the day.
6. It will be cloudy with sunny intervals.
7. There will be icy conditions on the roads in the morning.
8. There may be one or two light showers towards the end of the afternoon.
9. Early-morning mist in coastal areas will clear slowly.
10. With clear skies and a good chance of snow tomorrow over high ground, it's good news for skiers.

2 **Make collocations by finding the adjectives which go with these nouns. They are all in Exercise 1.**

a *heavy* rain, frost
b .... winds
c .... intervals
d .... conditions
e .... showers
f .... areas
g .... skies
h a .... chance
i .... ground
j .... news

Language tip

Note these collocations:

- heavy / light: rain, snow, frost(s), shower(s)
- strong / light: wind(s)

Writing and speaking

3 **Work in groups of four. Write a weather report for the next four days. Give the weather forecast to the rest of the class.**

Listening

46

4 **Listen to the conversation. What is the biggest difference between the weather where Anya lives and the weather in your country?**

5 **Listen again. Decide which statements are true and correct the false ones.**

- a It's often very cold at night in winter.
- b It occasionally snows in the mountains.
  F. It snows a lot in the mountains.
- c It frequently snows in the valleys from November through to March.
- d Thunderstorms happen most frequently in July and August.
- e It hardly ever rains in spring.
- f Anya can't remember a time when it rained more often than this spring.
- g Wildfires have sometimes happened in the past.
- h This year, fires have happened much more frequently than in the past.

Use of English Adverbs of frequency

(adverb) never
(adverb) hardly ever / rarely
(adverb) occasionally / sometimes
(adverb) often / frequently
(comparative adverb) more often / more frequently
(superlative adverb) most often / most frequently

6 **Read these questions. Give answer that are true for you. Use the appropriate adverbs of frequency.**

- a Does it ever snow where you live?
  No, it never snows. / Yes, sometimes.
- b How often are there storms with high winds and heavy rain?
- c Is there ever a risk of wildfires or floods?
- d Are there any weather conditions that happen more often now than in the past?
- e When do thunderstorms happen most frequently?

Speaking

7 **Work in pairs. Role-play an interview like the one in Exercise 4. Use the questions in Exercise 6. Practise the interview, then record it.**

8.2 Global warming and climate change

In this lesson you will...

- read about the causes and effects of global warming
- learn and use vocabulary for extreme weather conditions.

Key words: Environmental science

the atmosphere
drought
to evaporate
flood
heatwave
hurricane / cyclone / typhoon
moisture
rays
reflected
tornado

- **What is extreme weather?**

Reading

1 **Read the article. What does the diagram show?**

Heatwaves, floods, hurricanes, tornadoes and droughts are nothing new, but there have been a lot of them in recent years. Why?

In the last 50 years, the average global temperature has risen by 0.7 °C. Five of the warmest years on record have occurred since 2016. Most scientists believe that this global warming is one of the main reasons for the increase in extreme weather. If the average global temperature continues to rise, the consequences will be extremely serious.

As the Earth's oceans become warmer, more moisture evaporates into the air. The extra moisture in the air causes heavier rain, more storms and floods.

The rise in temperature makes dry areas with low rainfall even drier and can turn them into deserts.

What causes global warming? The Sun warms the Earth. Its rays pass through the Earth's atmosphere and they are reflected back out to space. The atmosphere is made of gases. Some of these are called 'greenhouse gases'. The gases form a protective layer that helps to control the heat passing to and from the Earth, and keeps it at the right temperature for animals, plants and humans.

Today, we use a lot of fuel to heat our houses, to drive our cars and to run our factories. This produces carbon dioxide (CO_2), which adds to the layer of gases in the atmosphere. The layer is getting thicker, and too much heat is kept in the Earth's atmosphere. Consequently, the Earth gets hotter, and that's when global warming becomes a problem.

Vocabulary

2 Match the words in the environmental science key words box to their definitions.

- a a large amount of water that covers an area which is normally dry
- b a long period of time when there is no rain
- c a very strong and dangerous wind that blows in a circle
- d a violent storm that forms over the land
- e higher than normal temperatures lasting for several days
- f the gases around the Earth
- g thin straight lines of light (from the Sun)
- h to change from a liquid into a gas
- i very small drops of water in the air
- j when light or heat is sent back out into space

3 Work with a partner. Answer the questions.

- a Why is there more interest today in extreme weather?
- b What has happened to the temperature of the Earth?
- c What's the connection between the oceans getting warmer and heavier rainfall?
- d What effect does global warming have on dry areas?
- e Why is the layer of gases round the Earth necessary?
- f What causes too much global warming?
- g Have there been any extreme weather conditions in your country in recent years? What were they?
- h Have you read or heard about any extreme weather conditions in the world in the last year? What were they? Where did they occur?

A forest fire

4 Work with a partner. Discuss how the photos relate to global warming. Then write a short paragraph about each one.

Ice is melting in the Arctic, making life difficult for wildlife like polar bears

8.3 I'm very concerned about ...

In this lesson you will...

- understand and express opinions about global environmental issues
- learn and use multi-word verbs connected with the environment.

- **What worries you most about the environment?**

Listening

47

1 Listen to Aisha, Raashid, Sana and Vinesh. What does each of them talk about?

- climate change
- depletion of resources
- non-renewable energy sources
- waste

2 Aisha, Raashid, Sana and Vinesh also expressed the following opinions, but they weren't recorded for the interviews. Who do you think gave each opinion?

a We should cut down on the number of new devices and appliances that we buy and try to recycle items that we don't use any more.

b We need to change the way we live so that we don't rely on burning fossil fuels. We're running out of time to make the changes we need to make.

c We should check that the clothes we wear are ethically produced. We have to think much more about living in a sustainable way and we have to stop being a 'throwaway' society.

d We must find ways of helping people who are suffering due to extreme weather conditions and disasters caused by global warming.

3 **Work in pairs. Write two sentences to summarise what each person talked about in Exercise 1.**

- Use the multi-word verbs from the Use of English box and words from the list below.

  Aisha is concerned about waste. She says we need to cut down on the amount we throw away.

  consume contaminate global warming
  digital / electronic appliances
  precious metals (gold, silver, platinum)
  renewable energy sources (solar, wind, hydro)

4 **Read the news story. Then answer the questions.**

a Which of the teenagers in Exercise 1 would be interested in this story and why?

b Would this idea work in your own community? Why / How?

Swapping fast fashion for a sustainable wardrobe

According to a recent survey, 60% of shoppers in the under-24 age group said they prefer to buy clothes from companies that are reducing their impact on the environment. Young consumers are keen to have a more sustainable approach to fashion and are shopping at stores that offer recycling schemes and free repairs. They are also using trading sites to resell and upcycle their clothes and footwear.

Use of English
Multi-word verbs

A **multi-word verb** contains a verb plus an additional word that is an adverb or a preposition. This combination gives it a specific meaning. For example, *call for* means 'make an official request or demand'.

We need to ***call for*** *action on reducing global warming before it's too late.*

Some multi-word verbs have two additional words. For example: *cut down on*, which means 'to reduce'.

We should ***cut down on*** *the number of new devices and appliances that we buy.*

Other multi-word verbs connected with the environment include:

cool down *look after*
run out of *throw away*
use up *wipe out*

Speaking

5 **Work in groups. Make a short video clip expressing your concerns about the environment and your ideas for sustainability.**

- Discuss the issues you think are most important. Ask questions to find out what students in your group are most concerned about, why they think it's a serious issue and what they suggest doing to solve the problem.
- Write a script for the video clip.
- Decide who is going to deliver each point.
- Rehearse your script.
- Make the video clip.

8.4 Zero waste

In this lesson you will...

- listen to suggestions for reducing waste
- use verbs followed by *-ing*.

- **Do you think it's possible to reduce your waste to zero?**

Reading

1 Read the text and look at the picture. Then answer the questions.

- **a** Why does Kathryn avoid buying packaged food and cleaning products?
- **b** How does Kathryn recycle green waste?
- **c** Why do you think Kathryn has become a zero-waste blogger?

Kathryn Kellogg has reduced her rubbish so much that now what she throws away over two years only fills a small container. She has done this by not buying packaged food and by making her own cleaning products. She also composts everything that is biodegradable*. This includes green waste, such as fruit and vegetable peelings, coffee grains and also paper and cardboard. She recycles everything that can be recycled. She is a zero-waste blogger: she encourages other people to reduce their waste by sharing her practical tips and suggestions online.

* Plants and materials made from plants, such as paper and cardboard, are 'biodegradable'. This means they decompose naturally and can be made into compost. Compost is used to improve the quality of soil for new plants to grow in.

Listening

48 **2 Listen to the audio for two short videos. What are the videos aiming to do?**

Vocabulary

3 **Work in pairs. Describe these items.**

bamboo	reusable	food container	bar	toothbrush
deodorant	shampoo	cardboard packaging	shopping bag	water bottle

a 

b 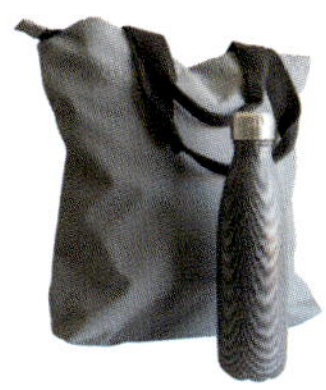

c 

d 

e 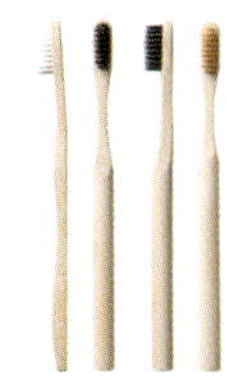

This is deodorant in cardboard packaging

4 **Read the questions about the advice you heard in Exercise 2. Write notes to answer them. Compare your answers with your partner's answers. Then listen again to complete them.**

a What advice is given about shopping and packaging?

b How do the items in the pictures help you to avoid buying single-use plastic?

c Why is it good for the environment to cut down on plastic?

d What kind of waste can you reduce by composting?

e What are the two advantages mentioned about shampoo in a bar?

f What advantages are mentioned about the deodorant?

5 **Choose a verb from the box to complete these sentences. Remember to use it in the *-ing* form.**

buy	use	reduce	make	recycle

a Discuss ***reducing*** waste with your family.

b Avoid ………… packaged food as much as possible.

c Stop ………… plastic bags.

d Consider ………… your own juices from fruit and vegetables.

e Keep ………… all your green waste, like fruit peelings and coffee grounds.

6 **Work in groups. Discuss the questions.**

a Why are people like Kathryn Kellogg keen on reducing waste?

b Which ideas in the audio in Exercise 2 do you agree with? Would you follow the advice?

Use of English
Verbs followed by *-ing*

These verbs are followed by the *-ing* form (not the *to* infinitive):

avoid	*consider*
discuss	*feel like*
give up	*imagine*
keep	*mention*
spend time	*suggest*

Avoid buying *single-use plastic as much as possible.*

Have you ***considered trying*** *a shampoo bar instead of shampoo that comes in a plastic bottle?*

8.5 Living and growing

In this lesson you will...

- read about growing food in cities
- discuss the advantages and disadvantages of urban farming.

Key words: Environmental science

consumer
food production
hydroponics
nitrogen
nutrient
supply chain
vertical farming

- **According to the United Nations, by 2050 2.5 billion more people will be living in cities. What kind of plans and changes do we need to make for city life in the future?**

Reading

1 **Read the text on the opposite page. Which title summarises it best?**

Parks and gardens in urban areas   Growing food in cities   Farming for the future

Vocabulary

2 **Read the text again. Find the words that mean:**

a finding another use for
b a small area of land, (here) for growing food
c a chemical substance used to kill viruses or insects on plants.

Speaking

3 **Work in pairs. Take turns to ask and answer the questions. Use the words from the environmental science key words box to help you.**

a Can you name four cities where people are growing vegetables on the roofs of buildings?
b What kind of fruit and vegetables are being grown?
c Why are old factories and empty warehouses being repurposed?
d What is hydroponics?
e How is transporting food made easier with urban farming?
f How do you think urban farming can reduce food waste?
g Where did the Aztecs grow food for the capital city's inhabitants?
h What did the Aztecs know about crops that grow well together?

4 Work in groups. Discuss the questions. Then exchange ideas with other groups.

a What are the advantages of urban farming and gardening for the environment?

b Are there any disadvantages?

c How do farming and gardening in the city help the people who live there?

Cities such as Shanghai, Singapore, Rotterdam and Paris are repurposing the roofs of office blocks, apartments and warehouses to make vegetable farms and gardens. Leafy green vegetables, soft fruits, herbs and salad crops are grown by urban farming companies. However, individuals can also rent a plot to grow their own food and local residents are encouraged to make gardens on their roofs.

It is not just rooftops that are being used for growing food. Old factories, empty warehouses and even abandoned underground transport tunnels have been converted to accommodate a system known as 'vertical farming'. Plants are grown inside without soil, using hydroponics. They receive the correct amount of light, water and nutrients. This means that less water and less space are needed than for growing the same crops outside on conventional farms. What's more, because the growing conditions are carefully controlled, pesticides are not necessary.

Vertical farming using hydroponics

Growing food in the city for the city is good for the environment. It's a much simpler supply chain and less food is wasted because produce is delivered quickly to consumers. Transport costs and emissions are also reduced.

Urban farming is not an entirely new idea. Over 500 years ago, one of the largest cities in the world at the time was Tenochtitlan (modern-day Mexico City), where more than 250,000 people lived. To feed the city, farmers grew crops on human-made floating islands called *chinampas*. The main crops were corn, beans and squash, which grow well together: the large leaves of the squash keep in moisture and keep weeds out. In addition, corn takes nitrogen from the soil, which beans then replace, so the main crops were grown in rotation. The Aztecs grew many other vegetables on their floating gardens, including tomatoes, avocados, chilli peppers, limes, peanuts and sweet potatoes. Willow trees were planted at the corners of the *chinampas* to anchor them to the bed of the lake below.

Organic salad crops being grown today on the floating islands made by the Aztecs

Farming and gardening help city dwellers to reconnect with food production. They also help them to value fresh food and healthy eating. Research suggests that trees and plants improve people's well-being and mental health. It seems that people who live near and have contact with plants and nature are healthier and happier.

8.6 The air we breathe

In this lesson you will...

- understand and discuss ideas about making cities sustainable for the future
- identify and use complex noun phrases.

- **Cities produce a lot of carbon emissions. Is this a problem? Why?**

Listening

Language tip

If something is 'sustainable' it means it can keep going now and in the future.

49

1 Listen to the conversation. How does Sania help her brother Nieran?

2 Listen again. Who mentions each of the following? Write 'S' for Sania or 'N' for Nieran.

a electric vehicles
b air quality
c public transport systems
d cycle routes
e pedestrianised zones
f low-emissions zones
g being socially and economically sustainable
h carbon neutral buildings
i renewable energy
j urban forests

3 Listen again. Then complete the notes Nieran wrote to prepare for the discussion.

a Make all cars and vehicles .... to avoid burning fossil fuels, and to improve ....

b Build good ...., so that people don't need to use their cars in the city.

c Have more .... zones because traffic-free, low-emissions zones encourage people to socialise and spend money. Consequently, cities are better places to live in and they are more 'socially and economically ....'.

d Plant more .... They can cool cities by between 2 and 8 degrees. They absorb a lot of ...., filter pollutants and particles and help to reduce flooding by soaking up .... through their roots.

e Children and adults can suffer when they don't have enough contact with the natural world, so having trees and other plants in cities improves .... and well-being.

Panama City seen from Soberanía National Park

Use of English Complex noun phrases

Complex noun phrases are useful for giving descriptions and information.

You can have ***low-emissions zones where people can enjoy going out and about.***

A noun phrase is a group of words that includes a noun and words that describe it.

A complex noun phrase can include a noun and:

- determiners and quantifiers *(the, this, my, one, a lot of)*: ***a lot of carbon***
- adjectives: ***a small electric car***
- relative clauses: ***zones where vehicles aren't allowed to go***
- prepositional and adverbial phrases: ***air conditioning in summer***.

Remember that a noun phrase or a complex noun phrase can be replaced by a pronoun:

- *an electric car = it*
- *good public transport systems = them*

It can also be the subject or the object of a verb.

The head noun in a noun phrase determines whether to use a singular or plural verb.

Renewable energy *from solar panels on city rooftops* ***helps*** *to reduce emissions from buildings.*

4 Identify the noun phrases in the sentences. (The questions in brackets will help you to identify them.)

a We're going to discuss <u>cities that are aiming to become more sustainable</u>. (What are we going to discuss?)

b Trees planted near rivers can reduce flooding. (What can reduce flooding?)

c They absorb a lot of carbon dioxide. (What do trees absorb?)

d Contact with the natural world is important for health and well-being. (What is important for health and well-being?)

e Those who have access to parks and green spaces tend to be happier. (Which city dwellers tend to be happier?)

Speaking

5 Work in pairs. Prepare for a discussion about how to make cities better places to live in. Talk about and write down your ideas.

I think having rooftop gardens for growing fruit and vegetables is a good idea. What do you think?

6 Work in groups. Have your discussion. Give reasons to back up your opinions. Use the information in Exercise 3 to help you. Be prepared to respond to other students' comments about your ideas. Think about what other people might say to oppose your points, for example:

That's all very well, but if everyone has electric vehicles, how will cities generate enough electricity?

Speaking tip

In a discussion:

- Give your own opinion and also ask other people what they think: *What do you think? What's your view? How do you see it?*
- Ask questions to clarify what someone else has said: *Are you saying that …? Do you mean that …?*
- Agree: *Yes, I agree. That's true. You've got a good point there. Exactly! Precisely! Definitely!*
- Disagree with an opinion: *That's an interesting point but … That's all very well but … I'm not convinced that …*

8.7 Improve your writing

In this lesson you will...

- write a report about extreme weather conditions.

1 **Read the report on the opposite page. Choose a heading for each of paragraphs a to d.**

On fire	Getting hotter more quickly in Australia	Summer heatwave	Then the rain came

2 **Answer the questions.**

a How does the headline get your attention?
b Why does the report have several paragraphs?
c Is the style of the report formal or informal? Is it descriptive or factual?
d What kind of detail does the writer include and why?
e Why do you think the writer includes a quote?
f Can you tell what the writer's own opinions are from the text?
g Where would you expect to read a report like this?
h Do you think the photo is a good choice to illustrate the report? Why? / Why not?
i What is the purpose of the photo caption?

3 **Write a report about weather conditions that have been in the news recently. Use the report about Australia as a model. Have you done the following?**

- written a good headline
- organised the information in short paragraphs
- included sub-headings for each paragraph
- included information and evidence
- written a conclusion for the final paragraph
- illustrated the report with a suitable image
- written a caption for the image.

Headline

Drought, bushfires and floods in Australia

Introduction

The summer of 2019–2020 was the second hottest on record in Australia. Temperatures were above average across almost the whole country.

a …………

Facts and figures

In December 2019, the heat was exceptional. The average temperature across the country was above 40 °C on 11 days in the month. On two consecutive days, 17 and 18 December, Australia recorded its hottest days on record. The heat continued through January and into early February.

b …………

More information

Detail

Quote

The extremely hot, dry conditions led to the worst bushfires in over 50 years. Low rainfall meant that moisture levels in the ground were very low. The fires burned 5 million hectares, destroying thousands of homes and wiping out wildlife. A resident of New South Wales said, 'Australia has always had bushfires, but the fires in 2019 were like nothing we'd ever seen before.'

c …………

Detail

Fortunately, rain started to fall in January and February 2020. In Sydney, there was more rain over four days than the city had had in the entire second half of 2019. In inland areas, the storms led to flash-flooding and rivers overflowed. However, some areas did not have enough rain to restore reservoir levels and ground water.

d …………

Conclusion

Scientists believe that the exceptional heat in summer is due to climate change and they are concerned that Australia's average temperatures are increasing more rapidly than in other parts of the world. Although the summer heat was followed by heavy rain, the driest parts of the country will continue to suffer from droughts.

Photo

Caption

Drought conditions in Victoria, Australia

8.8 Project challenge

Project 1: Sustainable living

You are going to compile and then present a list of your five favourite ideas for sustainable living.

1 Work in small groups. Brainstorm ideas. You could include any of the following or come up with ideas of your own:

- cutting down on single-use plastic
- avoiding non-biodegradable packaging
- composting green waste
- reducing emissions
- growing your own fruit and vegetables
- reusing, recycling, repurposing clothing, digital devices, etc.
- being a volunteer in a community project.

2 Decide which five ideas to include in your list.

3 Prepare the list for your presentation, giving reasons for your choices.

We think it's a good idea to try making your own fruit juices and smoothies. They'll be delicious and you'll avoid buying juices in plastic bottles from the supermarket.

Making your own fruit smoothies

4 Decide who is going to present each idea. Practise your presentation within the group. Do you need to consider making any changes or improvements? Are you going to show any pictures, photos or other items?

5 Give your presentation to the rest of the class. Ask for comments and feedback.

- Which do you think were the best ideas your group came up with?
- Did the other groups present any good ideas that you hadn't thought of? What were they?

Project 2: Sustainable city planning

You are going to make a plan for a sustainable future for your area.

Your city is going to redevelop an area near your school. The city council has invited you to present your ideas.

1 Work in groups. Read the list of instructions about the plan.

The old industrial area needs to be improved. The disused factories and empty warehouses will be repurposed or replaced for a sustainable future for the area and for the city. We are inviting the local community, including schools and colleges, to take part in planning the redevelopment. The following ideas are being considered. Please send us a list of five ideas, with reasons to support them. You can choose ideas from the list or add your own.

- A park with trees, grassy areas, benches and children's play equipment
- A sports centre with a swimming pool
- Cafés with indoor and outdoor seating
- Carbon-neutral apartment buildings
- Cinemas and concert rooms
- Office space, workshops and meeting rooms
- A public transport system station
- Recycling bins
- Renewable energy generation
- Rooftop gardens
- Safe cycle tracks around the area and a secure bike park facility
- Spaces for a variety of shops and small businesses
- Vertical farming areas.

2 What should the new area include? Which of the ideas from the list do you think are the best? Are there any ideas you would add?

3 Write your list of ideas, giving reasons to support each one.

- How did your work on lessons 1–6 in this unit help you to do this project?
- How might the work you have done on this project be useful to you in the future?

8.9 Poetry

Nadine Anne Hura is an author and journalist from New Zealand. She is of Māori descent on her father's side of the family. In the poem 'For Papatūānuku', she speaks to the Earth. She wrote it on 23 March 2020, when New Zealand was going into lockdown* because of the COVID-19 pandemic. *Papatūānuku* means 'Mother Earth' in Māori and the 'e' before it shows that the words are spoken directly to Papatūānuku.

* time during which people's movements are restricted for health or security reasons

50

1 Read and listen to the poem. How does it make you feel?

2 Read the poem again and answer the questions.

a In the first verse, the writer says, 'We'll not move upon you'. Why do you think she repeats the idea in lines 6–7? What do you notice about the sounds in the words she uses here: *cease*, *slow*, *stay*?

b Why do you think the word 'time' is repeated in lines 14–20?

c Why do you think the writer says in lines 22–23 that we should take off our shoes and touch the soil?

d Why do you think the writer mentions the wind, forests, oceans and rain?

e Why are 'grounding flights' and 'consumption' mentioned?

f What do you think the writer means by 'the concrete belt'?

1 *Papatūānuku*: Mother Earth
5 awhile: (literary) for a short time
12 *hei aha*: oh well, whatever
18 withhold judgment: to not give opinions
24 sift: (here) to let the soil fall through your fingers
25 gentle: calm, kind or soft
25 palm: the inside of your hand
35 *Ka turuturu te wai kamo o Rangi ki runga i a koe*: tears from the eyes of Ranginui drip down on you (Ranginui is 'Sky Father' in Māori culture)
37 embrace: to accept something with enthusiasm
38 sacrifice: giving something up that is valuable to you in order to help others
38 solitude: being alone
38 carve out: (here) to create something (as if making something by cutting into wood or stone)
40 *he iti noaiho*: something small
42 ground: to prevent from flying
43 consumption: buying and using things
51 absence: not being somewhere
52 loosen: to make something become loose
52 cinched tight: (here) fastened tightly
53 waist: part of the body above the hips
57 heal: to become well again after an illness or injury

For Papatūānuku

Rest now, e Papatūānuku
Breathe easy and settle
Right here where you are
We'll not move upon you
For awhile

We'll stop, we'll cease
We'll slow down and stay home

Draw each other close and be kind
Kinder than we've ever been.
I wish we could say we were doing it for you
as much as ourselves

But hei aha

We're doing it anyway

It's right. It's time.
Time to return
Time to remember
Time to listen and forgive
Time to withhold judgment
Time to cry
Time to think

About others

Remove our shoes
Press hands to soil
Sift grains between fingers

Gentle palms

Time to plant
Time to wait
Time to notice
To whom we belong

For now it's just you
And the wind
And the forests and the oceans and the sky
full of rain

Finally, it's raining!

Ka turuturu te wai kamo o Rangi ki runga
i a koe

Embrace it

This sacrifice of solitude we have carved out
for you

He iti noaiho – a small offering
People always said it wasn't possible
To ground flights and stay home and stop
our habits of consumption

But it was
It always was.

We were just afraid of how much it
was going to hurt – and it IS hurting
and it will hurt and continue to hurt
But not as much as you have been hurt.

So be still now

Wrap your hills around our absence
Loosen the concrete belt cinched
tight at your waist

Rest.
Breathe.
Recover.
Heal –

And we will do the same.

Nadine Anne Hura

Milford Sound, New Zealand

Moonlight, Summer Moonlight

'Tis moonlight, summer moonlight,
All soft, and still and fair;
The silent time of midnight
Shines sweetly everywhere,

But most where trees are sending
Their breezy boughs on high,
Or stooping low are lending
A shelter from the sky.

Emily Brontë

Emily Brontë

51

3 Read and listen to 'Moonlight, Summer Moonlight'. Then answer the questions.

- a What picture do you have in your mind when you read this poem?
- b Which words rhyme?
- c What do you notice about the rhythm of each line? (Clue: notice where the stress falls on each word.)
- d Why do you think Emily Brontë focuses on the trees in the second verse?
- e Why do you think she wrote the poem?

[1] 'Tis: (*literary*) it is
[6] breezy: windy
[6] bough: branch of a tree
[7] stooping: bending forwards towards the ground
[8] shelter: a place or structure that gives protection

Creative writing

4 Choose one of the following:

- Write a reply from Mother Earth to the poem 'For Papatūānuku'.
- Write a description of a scene from nature, such as a moonlit night, a frosty morning, a storm, snow falling, a heatwave.

Check your progress

General knowledge quiz

1 What is a heatwave?

2 What is the name of the kind of weather condition in which very strong winds move in circles and form over land?

3 What does the photo show? Why is it happening?

4 Why does increasing global warming lead to more frequent storms and floods?

5 Why are gases, such as CO_2, causing global warming?

6 If something is 'biodegradable', what happens to it?

7 If you were a 'zero-waste blogger', what would you write about?

8 What is 'vertical farming'?

9 What is the modern-day name of Tenochtitlan, the capital of the Aztec empire?

10 What were the three main crops the Aztecs grew on their floating islands?

Vocabulary

Weather

1 **Match the weather symbols to the descriptions.**

1  2  3  4 

5  6 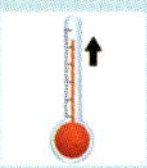 7  8 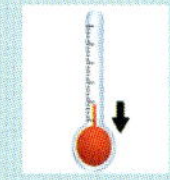

a cloudy with sunny intervals

b ice

c temperature falling

d temperature rising

e showers

f snow

g strong winds

h thunder and heavy rain

Sustainable cities

2 **Complete the sentences with the words from the box.**

pedestrianised zones	air quality
cycle routes	electric vehicles
renewable energy	

a People can walk around in .... but cars and other vehicles cannot enter them.

b Solar, wind and geothermal are sources of ....

c More people cycle to work when there are safe ....

d Poor .... in cities leads to ill-health and pollution.

e Only .... are allowed to enter some areas which are low-emissions zones.

Use of English

1 **Complete the sentences with the correct words.**

a We need to cut down ***on*** the amount of rubbish we throw away.

b We know that plastic waste in rivers and oceans is wiping .... fish and other species.

c We should look .... the things we have, so that we don't just buy things and then throw them away.

d The world is running .... of non-renewable energy sources such as oil and coal.

e The Earth and the oceans have got warmer and it's very unlikely that they will cool ....

2 **Complete the conversation with correct verb in the *-ing* form.**

do	make	try
reduce	remind	take

Saira: Can you imagine ....[1] your waste at home to zero?

Adya: Well, I've discussed ....[2] to cut down on plastic with my family.

Saira: Me too. And when we go to the supermarket, I keep ....[3] my parents to choose the things that come in biodegradable packaging.

Adya: That's good. I've considered ....[4] my lunch to school in a reusable container.

Saira: It's a great idea, but it means you'll have to spend time ....[5] the food to put in it.

Adya: Oh, that's OK. I'll just have to do it the night before. I won't feel like ....[6] it in the morning before school.

3 **Choose the correct verb form to match the underlined noun phrase in each sentence.**

a The air conditioning for the summer months ***use / uses*** a lot of electricity.

b Plans for a new public transport system ***is / are*** being considered.

c Low-emission zones in the city centre ***helps / help*** to improve air quality.

d The use of small electric cars in cities ***reduce / reduces*** congestion and pollution.

e A team of volunteers ***has / have*** planted 100 new trees in the park.

Summary checklist

I can

- ☐ talk about the weather and describe extreme weather conditions.
- ☐ understand what causes global warming and climate change.
- ☐ express opinions about global environmental issues.
- ☐ talk about reducing waste.
- ☐ discuss the advantages and disadvantages of urban farming.
- ☐ talk about ways of making cities sustainable for the future.
- ☐ write a report about extreme weather conditions.

9 Achievements and ambitions

In this unit you will...

- **do** a survey on the kinds of jobs teenagers would like to do
- **find out** about how a celebrity helped a young person achieve her dream
- **learn** about what you need to be good at for certain jobs
- **listen to** and **read** accounts of inspirational athletes
- **talk** about your plans and ambitions for the future
- **discuss** the achievements of young people
- **write** a letter to your 21-year-old self
- **give** a talk about the job you would like to do
- **read** about a girl who achieved her ambition.

Getting started

"What do you hope for in the next ten years?"

Watch this!

9.1 I'd like to be ...

In this lesson you will...

- listen to a conversation about a survey of the kinds of jobs teenagers would like to do, and do your own survey
- revise the use of relative clauses.

- **Is it important to think now about the kind of job you want to do in the future? Give reasons for your answer.**

Vocabulary

1 **Look at the chart. What kind of jobs do most UK teenagers want to do? What are the least popular jobs?**

This chart is based on a survey of over 7000 young people, aged between 14 and 18, in the UK. It shows their career aspirations.

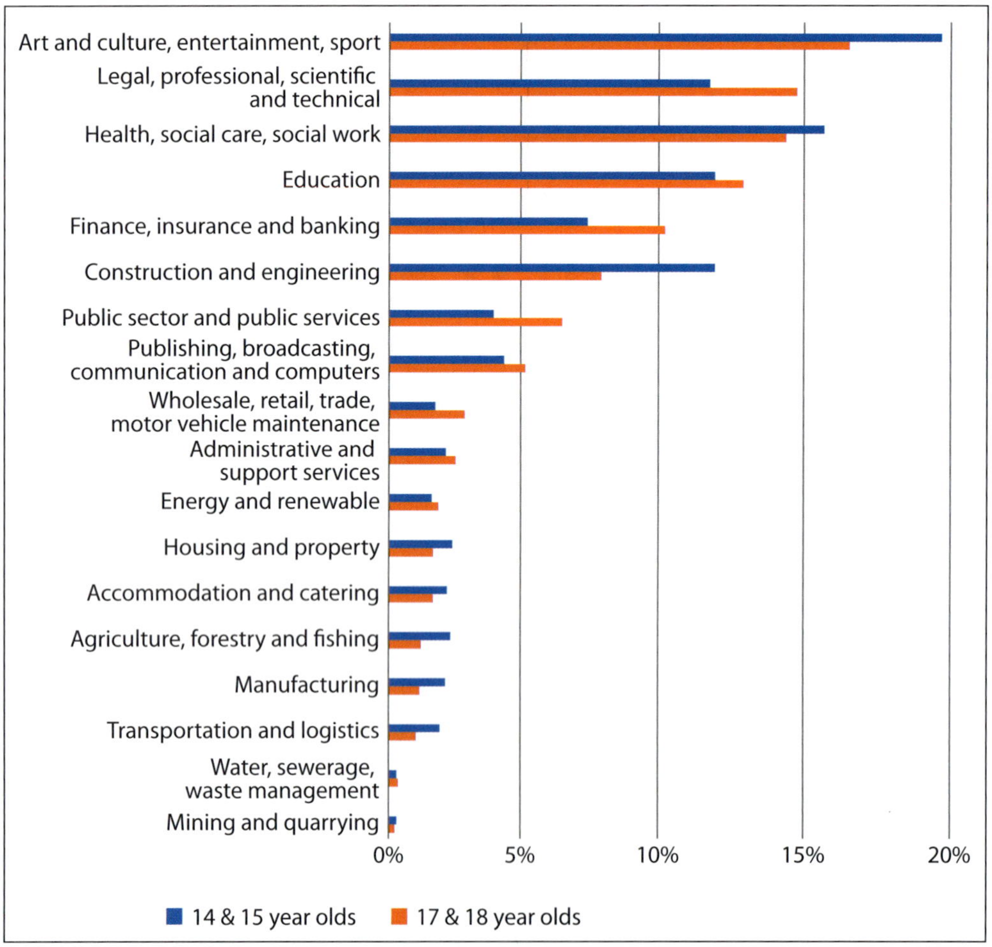

legal: to do with the law

the public sector: businesses and industries that are owned or controlled by the government

public services: services provided by the government (for example, schools, hospitals, the police)

broadcasting: television and radio

wholesale: selling goods in large amounts to shops and businesses

retail: selling goods to individuals

transportation: the movement of people or goods from one place to another

logistics: organising a complicated activity so that it happens in a successful and effective way

sewerage: the system of pipes and passages that carry waste material and used water away

mining: the process of getting minerals out of the ground

quarrying: the process of extracting material from the surface of the ground

Listening

52

2 **Listen to Esme and Abbas talking about the chart. At the end of the conversation, Esme says, 'But I thought you said earlier that you …'. Why does she say this? How might she continue?**

3 **Join these sentences with *who* or *which / that*.**

- **a** I've got a French friend. She works for an international bank.
- **b** I'd like to be a doctor. It's the career both my parents chose.
- **c** My uncle works for a transportation and logistics company. It helps people move to another country when they get a new job.
- **d** Working in a museum could be interesting, but you'd be in one room all day. That could be quite boring.

4 **Work with a partner. What examples of jobs do Esme and Abbas give? Write a list. Compare your list with the lists of other students.**

people who work in (testing laboratories)

people who work as (personal assistants)

people who work for (a bank, newspapers)

people who look after (others)

Remember
Relative clauses

In relative clauses, remember to use *who* for people and *which / that* for things.

Maybe it means scientists and people **who** *work in testing laboratories.*

You mean estate agents, **who** *help you to buy and sell a house or a flat.*

Retailers sell the fruit **which** *they have bought from the wholesalers.*

And remember that you can use *which* to refer to the whole of a previous clause.

I wouldn't have to worry about being unemployed, **which** *would be very nice.*

Speaking

5 **Look at the chart in detail and discuss this question: What are the differences between the two groups of teenagers?**

More of the younger / older teenagers would like to work in …

I think that's surprising.

I don't find it surprising, because …

6 **Do the survey in your own class. Ask about each category.**

Who would like to work in art and culture, entertainment or sport?

What would you like to be?

Record the results. If you have a chance to ask older students the same questions, record the results and compare them.

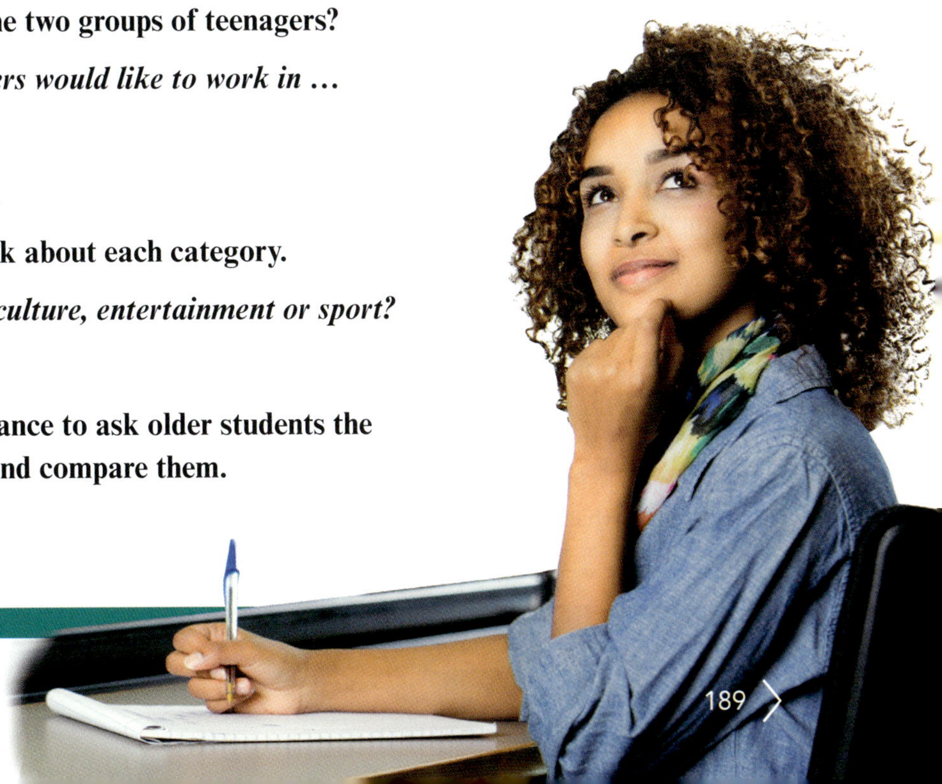

9.2 I'm over the moon!

In this lesson you will...

- find out about how a celebrity helped a young person achieve her dream
- discuss other stories of how well-known people have helped others.

- **Does everyone have the same opportunity to study at university or college?**

Reading

1 **Read the article. Who are the two people in the photos?**

Writing

2 **Work in pairs. Without looking at the article, each student uses the words in the economics key words box to write a summary of it. Try to use *However* and *although* in your summary. Can you also include *out of the blue* and *over the moon*? When you have finished, compare your summaries.**

3 **Answer the questions.**

a What was the problem that Vitoria faced?
b What sort of 'general living costs' might Vitoria have at university?
c What impressed Taylor Swift about Vitoria's story?
d Why does the journalist say that Vitoria 'has achieved so much'?
e What is the journalist's impression of Vitoria?

Speaking

4 **Work in groups. Think of other examples of famous people (musicians, actors, film stars, business people) who have given money to help other people. Describe what they have done, without naming them. The other members of the group have to say who the person is.**

Language tip

Idiomatic language

Remember that using idiomatic language can make your spoken language or informal written language more colourful.

Vitoria says that Taylor Swift's message came 'out of the blue'. What does she mean? And what does she mean when she says she was 'over the moon'?

Key words: Economics

afford to
charity
fundraising
living costs
raise money
social mobility
student loan

Remember Connectives

Find these connectives in the article:

although However

Although is used to balance two contrasting clauses:

*Her family could not afford to support her, **although** they really wanted her to have a university education.*

or

***Although** her family could not afford to support her, they really wanted her to have a university education.*

However usually comes after a full stop or a semicolon.

*In four years, she has achieved so much. **However**, she still has ambitions.*

Vitoria Mario, an 18-year-old student from north London, wanted to go to university to study maths. She had achieved remarkably good results in her A-level exams – two A-stars in maths and further maths and an A in physics – but to go to university she would have to pay for accommodation and general living costs, as well as textbooks and a laptop. Her family could not afford to support her, although they really wanted her to have a university education.

At the age of 13, Vitoria had come to London to live with an uncle, because her mother, who still lives in Portugal, wanted her to have the best chance of getting to university. This meant that Vitoria didn't have 'home' status in the UK, so she was not able to get a student loan from a bank.

However, she was determined to raise the money in order to achieve her dream, so she emailed 442 people in companies across the country and sent letters to people explaining her situation, but she had no responses. She was ready to give up, but she decided to set up an online fundraising page on the internet, explaining her situation.

'My dream of becoming a mathematician,' she wrote, 'is not only a chance for social mobility for my family and me, but also to inspire people who have been in similar positions to aspire to be the best version of themselves and strive for their dreams.'

Imagine her surprise when she received a message from Taylor Swift, a singer-songwriter who has sold more than 50 million albums and 150 singles worldwide.

The message said: 'Vitoria, I came across your story and am so inspired by your drive and dedication to turning your dreams into reality. I want to gift you the rest of your goal amount. Good luck with everything you do! Love, Taylor.'

The message from Taylor Swift had come 'out of the blue', said Vitoria. 'I was wondering how to reach enough people to hit my goal and now this miracle has happened ... I'm just over the moon!'

Vitoria now has a place at the University of Warwick to study maths.

When Vitoria arrived in the UK, she couldn't speak English. In four years, she has achieved so much. However, she still has ambitions.

'I want to encourage females to do science subjects. In my school, I'm the only girl doing maths at university. My goal is to create a charity that helps people like me.'

9.3 Would you be good at ...?

In this lesson you will...

- learn about what you need to be good at for certain jobs
- learn to detect bias in what people write or say.

Remember

Remember that 'bias' is when someone allows personal opinions to influence the way they see things or their judgement.

- **For which jobs do you need to be good at looking at the facts and finding evidence?**

Reading and listening

1 **Here are two witness statements. Are they about the same incident or two different incidents?**

A

It was around 9 o'clock on Tuesday evening. I was making my way home along Delancey Street. There weren't many people around. I noticed a young man coming towards me, in the distance. He was smartly dressed, in a nice suit. Suddenly, out of the blue, this other man appeared from a side street by Thornton's Café, went right up to him, and started a conversation with him. It looked as if he was having a heated argument with him. And then he pointed his finger at the first man. The first man looked frightened and lost his balance. I didn't want to get involved but I thought I'd better report it, especially as there have been several incidents in the area recently, with all these new people moving into the area. I felt a surge of anger, but I couldn't do anything. The second man looked like a motorcyclist. He was broad-shouldered and he was wearing a leather jacket and jeans. You see a lot of them in this area. They're annoying and irresponsible. People going about their business these days just aren't safe.

B

I'd just watched the news on TV, so it was between 9.15 and 9.20. My flat is just above Thornton's Café, on the corner of Delancey Street and Lyle Street. It was quite dark, but there was enough light from the sign above the café for me to see what was happening. I was standing at the open window. I could see a man walking towards the café, along Delancey Street. He was wearing a light blue suit, he had fair hair and he was carrying an umbrella. I could see him clearly, as he was facing me. I'd say he was in his thirties. As he got to the café, another man walking down Lyle Street reached the same point. He asked the first man the time. I could hear clearly what he said. The first man answered him quite rudely, saying, 'If you think I'm going to get my phone out to tell you the time, you must be joking.' He raised his umbrella. Up to that point, the second man had stood at a distance from the first man, but he then went towards him, shrugged his shoulders and made a gesture as if to say 'I don't know what you mean.' He walked away. I only saw the back of the second man, so I am not able to give a full description of him, apart from saying that he was tall and broad-shouldered.

53

2 **Listen to two students discussing the statements. Can they detect bias in one or both of the statements?**

54

3 **Listen to Karina and Alexander discussing three candidates for a job. Can you detect bias in what either of them says?**

Vocabulary

4 **Complete these collocations from Exercises 1 and 3.**

Exercise 1

to ***make*** your way home
to go .... up to someone
to have a .... argument with someone
to .... your finger at
the man .... his balance
to .... about your business
up to that ....
to shrug your ....

Exercise 3

we've got a ....list of three candidates
he's got great .... charm
he's a digital ....
it was a .... achievement
a .... player
to .... the part
from our .... of view

Use of English Participle clauses

In the sentence 'I noticed a young man coming towards me', the word *coming* is a present participle. It introduces a clause: 'coming towards me'.

Participle clauses can replace relative clauses in some sentences.

present participle
I noticed a young man ***coming*** *towards me.* = I could see a young man who was coming towards me.

present participle
People ***going*** *about their business just aren't safe these days.* = People who are going about their business just aren't safe these days.

Language tip

Remember, collocations are words that are often found together. Examples from the witness statements in Exercise 1 are *a surge of anger* (NOT ~~an increase~~ *of anger*) and *broad-shouldered* (NOT ~~wide~~-*shouldered*).

5 **Rewrite these sentences using participle clauses.**

a I could see a man who was walking towards the café.
b The other people who work in that department are young.
c She worked for a publishing company that specialised in art books.
d She was the one who was wearing jeans and a leather jacket.

Writing and speaking

54

6 **Work in groups. Listen again to Karina and Alexander discussing the candidates for the design job in Exercise 3. Make notes on the three candidates, A, B and C. Then discuss them and decide who is going to get the job.**

9.4 Achieving your dreams

Tegla Loroupe

In this lesson you will...

- listen to and read accounts of inspirational athletes
- use reported speech.

- **How can sport make a difference to people's lives?**

Listening

55

1 Listen to the interview with a sports journalist.
Who is Tegla Loroupe? Why is she the focus of the podcast?

Vocabulary

2 Complete the sentences with the correct words.

An ambassador A mentor A refugee A world champion	is someone who	**a** gives another person help and advice over a period of time. **b** has beaten all other competitors in a sport. **c** officially represents a country, or an organisation. **d** has had to leave their country to escape from conflict or for economic reasons.

3 Summarise the interview using the words in Exercise 2 and the words and phrases from the list below.

Kenya	from the age of 6	races	runner	in bare feet
marathon	leaders	tribes	conflicts	the Olympics

Listening

56

4 Listen to information about two members of the Refugee Olympic Team, Yusra Mardini and Aker Al Obaidi. Note which of the words in the list relate to Yusra and which to Aker.

Austria	boat	German	Germany	Iraq
scholarship	swimming	Syria	wrestling	

"Competing at the Olympics has been a dream of mine since I was a young girl."

5 **First read the questions. Make notes to answer them. Then listen again and complete your answers.**

a Where is Yusra from?

b Why were Yusra and her sister travelling in 2015 and what happened on their journey?

c Which country did Yusra go to?

d How did she get to compete at the Olympics in Rio de Janeiro?

e Where is Aker Al Obaidi from and why did he have to leave home?

f Which country did he reach?

g What sport does he do?

h How has the International Olympic Committee helped him?

i Why do Yusra and Aker want to continue competing in their sports?

"It is my goal. It's the biggest dream, to compete at an Olympics, and because I don't have a nationality right now, it would be great to show that refugees can compete and succeed, too."

6 **Decide who said the following, Yusra Mardini or Aker Al Obaidi. Then report what each person said.**

a 'I've made some good friends in Austria.'
Aker Al Obaidi said he had …

b 'The journey from Syria to Europe was very hard.'

c 'I've been given a scholarship by the IOC.'

d 'I'm enjoying life in Germany but I miss my home country.'

e 'I was taking part in wrestling matches before I left Iraq.'

Use of English Reported speech: statements (revision)

In reported speech:

- present simple changes to past simple

  *'My family **are** very proud of me.'*

  Aker Al Obaidi said his family **were** very proud of him.

- present continuous changes to past continuous

  *'I'**m enjoying** my sport.'*

  He said he **was enjoying** his sport.

- past simple changes to past perfect (or can stay in past simple)

  *'We **decided** to leave Syria after our house was destroyed.'*

  Yusra and her sister said they **had decided** to leave Syria after their house **was** destroyed.

- present perfect changes to past perfect

  *'Competing at the Olympics **has been** a dream of mine since I was a young girl.'*

  Yusra said competing at the Olympics **had been** a dream of hers since she was a young girl.

- past continuous changes to the past perfect continuous.

  *'I **was training** for swimming competitions in Syria.'*

  She said she **had been training** for swimming competitions in Syria.

Speaking

7 **Work in pairs. Use the questions and your answers in Exercise 5 to role-play two interviews for a podcast between the presenter and a sports journalist.**

Presenter: ***Hello and welcome to this series which features amazing people. Today, I have sports journalist (your partner's name) in the studio and we're going to talk about Yusra Mardini. First of all, where is she from?***

9.5 The power of the mind

In this lesson you will...

- read and discuss an article about the science behind positive thinking
- talk about your own plans and ambitions for the future.

- **How do you use the power of your mind? When and how does positive thinking help you?**

Reading

1 **Read the text on the opposite page. Would you describe it as mainly fact-based, mainly opinion-based or a mixture of the two? Why?**

2 **Work in pairs. Use the terms in the medical science and psychology key words box to discuss these questions.**

a How do positive experiences affect your brain?
b How does stress affect your health?
c What can you do to reduce feelings of stress and anxiety?
d How can thinking about the future make you feel happier now?
e What else should you do to feel more positive?
f What should you avoid doing?

3 **Work in groups. Discuss the questions.**

a Is it always an advantage to be optimistic? Why / Why not?
b What kind of things do you feel pessimistic about? Why do you think this is?
c Which pieces of advice from the text in Exercise 1 do you think are most helpful for you? Why?

Language tip

Remember:

- Use the future *will* for predictions of what you think or guess will happen: *Do you usually expect that things* ***will turn out*** *well?*
- Use the future continuous to say that something will be in progress at a time in the future: *Thinking about what you* ***will be doing*** *in the future can have a strong impact on your present state of mind.*
- *I hope that, ten years from now, I* ***will be studying*** *to be a doctor.*

Reading tip

How to tell the difference between fact and opinion:

- A **fact** refers to something that is true. It can be verified with evidence that proves it is true.
- In the first paragraph, the writer refers to 'recent studies' that have found evidence about optimism, so this is factual information.
- An **opinion** is a personal belief. It shows what someone feels about something. You can agree or disagree with an opinion, but you can't prove or disprove it.
- In the second paragraph, the writer gives examples of 'activities that are enjoyable, such as sports and games'. This is an opinion. Some people wouldn't agree that taking part in sports and games is enjoyable.

Speaking

4 **Work in pairs. Visualise what you will be doing ten years from now. What are the first three ideas you think of? Compare your ideas with your partner. Ask questions to continue the conversation.**

Where will you be living?

Where will you be working / studying?

What do you think you'll be doing in your free time?

Are you an optimist or a pessimist? Do you usually expect that things will turn out well or do you think about the possible problems and difficulties ahead? Recent studies have shown that optimism is 50% inherited through our genes, 40% determined by ourselves and 10% influenced by our environment. That's good news, because it means we can work on the 40% to increase our levels of optimism.

The human brain reacts to positive experiences by releasing chemicals such as dopamine, serotonin, oxytocin and endorphins. These chemicals produce positive emotions. Consequently, taking part in activities that are enjoyable, such as sports and games, and spending time with friends and family, will increase the release of brain chemicals, which in turn will make you feel happier and more positive.

On the other hand, researchers believe that negative emotions can weaken the immune system. Stress causes physical reactions in the body, which can raise blood pressure and blood sugar levels. But techniques such as controlled breathing and relaxation can help to reduce feelings of anxiety.

According to a study by the University of Kansas, smiling, even if you don't feel like smiling, reduces your heart rate and lowers blood pressure in stressful situations.

There is evidence that thinking about what you will be doing in the future can have a strong impact on your present state of mind. A study published in the Journal of Genetic Psychology found that children who saw themselves in the future doing work they liked and having a happy life had higher levels of self-esteem than other children.

The study also found that techniques such as visualising what you want to happen or writing down your ideas and plans for the future were helpful. It advised being more aware of thoughts, moods and emotions and being less self-critical. It recommended thinking about yourself in a positive but realistic way, valuing the positive aspects of your life and not getting into the habit of complaining about people or situations.

Key words: Medical science and psychology

- blood pressure
- blood sugar levels
- chemicals (dopamine, serotonin, oxytocin, endorphins)
- heart rate
- immune system
- lower
- raise
- release
- self-critical
- self-esteem
- value
- visualise
- weaken

9.6 Young achievers

In this lesson you will...

- discuss the achievements of young people
- learn and use adjectives with dependent prepositions.

- **Who do you think of as a young achiever and why?**

Reading

1 Read about three teenagers. Then answer the questions.

Laura Dekker, a teenager from the Netherlands, sailed around the world by herself at the age of 15. She had been sailing with her father since she was very young and he knew she was capable of sailing on her own, even in difficult and dangerous conditions. The trip took 74 weeks.

Jacob Barnett has been interested in maths and physics since he was a small child. At the age of ten, he started studying astrophysics at university in Indiana, USA. In his spare time, he earned money by tutoring fellow students in advanced mathematics. He is autistic. He gave a TED talk on creative thinking, which has become one of the most watched TED talks of all time.

Kelvin Doe is a young inventor from Sierra Leone. When he was 13, he was so fed up with the poor electricity supply to his neighbourhood that he built a generator and batteries to provide power to his family's house and to the surrounding homes. He used pieces of metal, wires and other materials that he found in rubbish bins.

a What do they have in common?

b What do you find surprising about each person?

c Which of the teenagers do you think has achieved the most? Why?

2 Work in pairs. Choose three adjectives to describe each person. Justify your choices.

ambitious curious inventive brave determined optimistic
capable fearless skilful confident intelligent unusual creative

Listening

57

3 Listen to Indah and Reza working on a presentation. What is the topic of the presentation? What surprises Indah about Reza?

4 Answer the questions.

a Why do Indah and Reza talk about the teenagers in Exercise 1? What do they find remarkable about them?

b What does Indah say about what she has achieved?

c What does Reza say will be a big achievement for him?

d What is their personal message for the presentation?

Use of English Dependent prepositions following adjectives

Some adjectives are followed by certain prepositions. There are no grammatical rules about this. It's best to learn them together. You already know several of them: *good at*, *interested in*, *afraid of*. Some adjectives can be followed by more than one preposition.

nervous about something, **about** doing something

worried, concerned about someone / something, **about** doing something

angry, annoyed about something / **with** someone

bored, fed up with something (also **of**)

proud of someone / something

capable of something / **of** doing something

different from something / someone

free, protected from something

similar to something / someone

polite to someone

good to someone / **for** you ('Sugary drinks aren't good for you')

kind, nice to someone / **of** you ('That's kind / nice of you')

grateful, thankful to someone / **for** something ('I'm grateful to you for your help')

famous, sorry for something / **for** doing something

satisfied, familiar with something

5 Complete each sentence with an adjective and preposition.

a I was so .... my brother for taking my bike without asking that I didn't speak to him for a whole day.

b It was very .... you to help me with my homework.

c This fruit juice is .... added sugar so it's very healthy.

d You needn't have been so .... the test. It was very easy.

Speaking

6 Work in pairs or groups. Ask and answer.

a What are you proud of?

b What would you like to be famous for?

c What do you think you will be most thankful for in ten years' time?

9.7 Improve your writing

In this lesson you will...

- write an informal letter.

1 **You are going to write a letter to your 21-year-old self. You are then going to put it in a safe place and only open it when you are 21.**

2 **On the opposite page is a model of a letter you could write. Read it. What do you think you will be doing when you are 21? Where will you be living?**

3 **Number these topics in the order they appear in the letter:**

- Free-time activities
- People you know
- Studies and work
- Talents and ambitions
- Trips to other countries

4 **Work with a partner. Look at the options that are underlined in the letter. Do any of them apply to you? Discuss them with your partner.**

Do you think you will go to university or college?

Yes, I'd like to. You once said you wanted to be a lawyer. Do you think you will study law?

I've changed my mind. I think I'd like to be a doctor, so I'd like to study medicine.

5 **Now write your own letter.**

- Use the letter on the opposite page to help you.
- Choose or change the underlined words to make them true for you.
- Read your letter carefully to check the spelling, punctuation and grammar.
- Show your letter to a classmate and ask for comments.
- Include any changes your classmate suggests and write your final version.
- Keep the letter and read it again when you are 21.
  You'll see if you have achieved your aims or changed your plans.

6 **Check that you have followed the instructions in Exercise 5.**

7 **If you would like an extra challenge, imagine you are 21 years old. You open the letter you wrote in this lesson and read it. Write a reply.**

Thanks for your letter. Yes, I'm now 21! I'm at university in …, where I'm just coming to the end of my course in …

Dear …

How are you? I hope things are going well for you. You will be 21 when you read this. I wonder what you will be doing and where you will be living. I can only guess!

Are you at university or college? If you are, are you studying (law / science / journalism), as you had hoped? What's your favourite part of the course? Are you still thinking of becoming a (lawyer / research scientist / journalist) when you've finished your degree? If you didn't go to university or college, what did you do?

When you were in Year 9, you were interested in (music / photography / martial arts). Do you still have time to (play the guitar / take photographs / do karate)? Have you got any new interests?

Have you done any travelling? I know that you had always dreamed of going to (New Zealand / South America / Alaska). Have you been there yet on holiday or are you hoping to (go travelling / get a job) there in the future?

You were also quite good at (sports / art / technology) when you were at school, and you once said that it was your ambition to (take part in the Olympics / have an exhibition of your work / invent and build a robotic device). Is that still true for you?

Do you remember (Alana) in Year 9? She was brilliant at (maths / science / everything). I wonder what she is doing now. Are you still in touch with her? Perhaps she (is a maths teacher / is training to be an astronaut / works for a computer software company.)

Best wishes

(your name)

9.8 Project challenge

Project 1: Your future job

You are going to give a short talk about the job you would like to do in the future.

1 Write a list of jobs you think you would like to do.

2 Work in pairs. Ask and answer the questions.

- Which of the jobs on your list do you think you would be best at? Why?
- Which of the jobs do you think you would find the most interesting? Why?

3 Decide which job you are going to talk about. Then think about the following:

- What sort of person do you need to be?
- How can the things you are doing at school now help you achieve your ambition?
- Do you need a university degree to do this job?
- What qualifications do you need?
- What other skills do you need?
- How long is the training?
- Is the job well paid?
- What are the good things about the job?
- Are there any disadvantages?
- Where do you see yourself in ten years' time?

4 Prepare your talk.

- Write a list of points to talk about.
- Rehearse what you will say for each point.
- Find visual images to show on screen to illustrate your talk if you want to.

5 Give your talk. Ask the class for comments and questions.

Has anyone got any questions?

- How did this project help you to think about jobs in the future?
- What did you learn from the talks your classmates gave?

Project 2: A discussion

You are going to organise a discussion about achievement.

1 Organise your group.

- Choose a chairperson to organise the discussion.
- Choose a secretary to write down the key ideas.
- Choose a spokesperson to summarise and present your group's ideas to the class.

2 Start by brainstorming ideas to answer the question: *What is achievement?*

- You can listen again to the conversation in Exercise 3 in Lesson 9.6 to get you started.
- Take turns to give your views on what achievement is.
- Give examples of people who have achieved their ambitions.
- Take turns to talk about personal achievements.

3 Evaluate the ideas.

- Make sure you consider all the ideas carefully.
- You are answering an open-ended question that has many possible answers, so don't make judgements too quickly.
- Choose the best ideas and summarise them.

4 Present your ideas to the rest of the class.

Language tip

Useful phrases

That's a good idea.

I agree with … because …

I disagree with … because …

Do you think that …?

How about …?

Did you mean …?

Can you give an example of that?

So what you're saying is …

I'd like to go back to what … said about …

Couldn't it also be that …?

- What did you find most interesting, surprising or useful about the discussion?
- How will your experience of doing this project help you in the future?

9.9 Fiction

***Rickshaw Girl* by Mitali Perkins**

I wrote *Rickshaw Girl* first as a tribute to my grandmothers, who were both girls in Bangladesh, the country bordering India to the east. Like most girls in Bangladesh, my grandmothers were skilled at painting *alpana*, a thousand-year-old decorative art found throughout the villages.

In *Rickshaw Girl*, my main character Naima is also an expert *alpana* artist. Girls mix rice powder with spices to create colourful symmetrical decorations for thresholds and doorways. But that's not the only places Bangladeshis decorate. The main mode of transport is the cycle rickshaw, a cart pulled by a bicycle. It's the taxi of the villages, carrying kids to school and goods to the markets. Even though most rickshaw drivers are quite poor, they splurge on beautiful paintings to adorn their rickshaws.

Mitali Perkins

58

1 **Read the summary of the story so far. Then read and listen to the extract. What is Naima's mother worried about and why?**

2 **Read the extract again and answer the questions.**

a Why is Naima glad that her sister is too far away to hear their parents' conversation? (lines 3–5)

b Why does Naima's mother say, "If only *one* of our girls had been a boy!" (line 9)? How do you think Naima might have felt?

c How would you describe the father's attitude towards Naima and Rashida?

d Is Rashida older or younger than Naima? How do you know?

e Naima's mother says, "*alpanas* can't put rice on the table" (line 17). What does she mean?

f Why do you think Naima scrubs out her *alpana* design?

g Do you think Naima agrees with her mother that 'all that a girl could do was cook, clean, wash clothes and decorate' (lines 25–26)? *Rickshaw Girl* was written as a tribute to the author's grandmothers. How might views such as this have changed over time?

3 **Work with a partner. Discuss these questions.**

a Which words and phrases in the extract tell you about Naima's character?

b Why does the writer use the adjectives 'plump', 'rich-looking' and 'juicy' in the final paragraph?

The story so far

Naima is the central character of the story. She lives with her mother, father and sister Rashida. Their next-door neighbour is Saleem, who is the same age as Naima. Naima's father and Saleem's father are rickshaw drivers. Naima's father has just come home from work ...

Mother's worried voice drifted through the open door: "How much did you earn this morning, Husband?"

Naima tried not to listen, but she couldn't help it. She was glad Rashida was stooping over the marigolds in the back, too far away to hear.

"Not enough," Father replied.

Mother's sigh sounded like air leaking from a tyre. Naima counted to five. She braced herself for words she'd overheard before. "If only *one* of our girls had been a boy!" Mother said.

Father gave his usual quick answer. "I have two wonderful daughters. They're just as good as boys."

"But you look so tired! Saleem takes his father's rickshaw out every afternoon so his father can rest. Our girls can't do that for you."

"Isn't Naima the best *alpana* painter in the village?" Father asked. "Doesn't she take care of her sister like a tiger guarding a cub? And Rashida is the best student in school!"

"Yes, but *alpanas* can't put rice on the table. And what use is it if Rashida is smart? We can't afford her school fees next year unless we pay off that rickshaw loan."

Rashida was coming back. Naima dunked the rag in the half-empty pail of water her sister was carrying. Fiercely, she scrubbed out her *alpana* design until no traces of the rice powder remained on the threshold.

"What are you doing, Sister?" Rashida asked. "You weren't finished! That was the best one yet!"

Naima didn't answer. Mother was right. All that a girl could do was cook, clean, wash clothes, and decorate; she wasn't allowed to do any work that brought in money. Painting *alpanas* wouldn't help Father get rest. Or add to their earnings. It was a waste of time.

"Rash-ee-da! Na-ee-ma! Come inside! Your father is hungry."

Saleem drove by again. This time a plump passenger sat on the bench of the rickshaw. He was a rich-looking passenger, juicy with money. Naima scowled and followed her sister into the hut.

1 **drifted:** moved slowly as if carried by the wind

4 **stooping:** bending forward and down

4 **marigolds:** plants with bright yellow or orange flowers

7 **sigh:** a slow breath out which makes a long soft sound

7 **leaking:** coming out from a small hole

7 **tyre:** a thick rubber ring that fits around the wheel of a car, bicycle or other vehicle

8 **braced herself:** prepared herself for something unpleasant

8 **overheard:** heard what someone was saying to someone else, not to you

14 ***alpana*:** a pattern painted in the doorway of a house, using rice-powder paint

18 **smart:** clever

18 **school fees:** money you pay to go to school

19 **loan:** money you borrow

20 **dunked:** put something into a liquid and took it out again

20 **pail:** bucket

21 **scrubbed out:** rubbed out so that it disappeared

22 **traces:** a very small amount of something

22 **threshold:** the floor of an entrance

30 **plump:** quite fat

32 **scowled:** looked angrily

4 **Work in groups. Read how the story continues and discuss the question below.**

> **What happens next**
>
> In order to help her family, Naima dresses as a boy so that she can drive the rickshaw while her father sleeps. However, she crashes the rickshaw, which means that the family is in even more trouble financially.
>
> Naima learns of a rickshaw repair shop in a nearby town so she dresses as a boy again and goes to the shop on the rickshaw. She's surprised to find that the person who owns the shop is a woman. She reveals that she is in fact a girl, and the woman hires her to paint *alpanas* on her rickshaws in return for doing repairs on Naima's father's rickshaw. The woman promises Naima that she can become an apprentice at the workshop in order to learn how to repair rickshaws herself.
>
> When her father eventually finds Naima, he is angry at first but then is proud of his daughter for becoming so independent.

Did Naima do the right thing? Give your reasons.

Creative writing

5 **Choose one of the following tasks.**

a Write a dialogue between Naima and the owner of the rickshaw shop, based on the second paragraph of the **What happens next** text.

b Look at the final paragraph of the text. Write the conversation that Naima and her father had when he found her.

Check your progress

General knowledge quiz

1 What subject would you study in order to work in the legal profession?

2 If someone works in 'retail', what do they do?

3 What is the connection between Taylor Swift and a teenager from London who set up a fundraising page on social media?

4 What do you do if you work in 'Human Resources'?

5 Who is Tegla Loroupe and why has she become an ambassador for world peace?

6 Which language is spoken in Austria?

7 What are dopamine, serotonin, oxytocin and endorphins?

8 This system helps the body fight against disease. What is it called?

9 The IOC is an important committee in the sports world. The I stands for 'International' and the C stands for 'Committee'. What does the O stand for?

10 It's a cart pulled by a bicycle and it's used as a taxi. What is it?

Vocabulary

Jobs and professions

1 **Match the jobs to the job areas.**

1	Agriculture	a	doctor / nurse
2	Art and culture	b	farmer
3	Health	c	lawyer
4	Legal	d	museum curator
5	Scientific	e	research scientist

Personality

2 **Choose the adjectives from the list to describe the person.**

brave confident creative curious determined optimistic unusual

Someone who:

a usually thinks positively about the future is …………

b is prepared to do something that might be dangerous is …………

c wants to find out new things is …………

d never gives up is …………

e does things that few other people do is …………

f feels that he / she can achieve a successful outcome is …………

g is good at thinking of different ideas and ways of doing things is …………

Use of English

1 **When Maia was asked about her plans for the future, this is what she said:**

> 'I've been thinking about jobs recently, because it's time to choose my options for Year 10. My mum found a survey online about jobs. I was thinking about social work, because I want to do something useful. Mum said that can be quite hard, and it's not well paid, so I'm now thinking about a career in medicine. I want to do a job in which I'm helping people.'

Report what Maia said. Start like this:

Maia said that she'd been thinking about …

2 **Maia did an online survey about personality types. Complete what she wrote with the correct prepositions.**

a I'm not nervous .... taking responsibility.

b I'm capable .... working hard.

c If I'm doing something difficult, I don't give up until I'm satisfied .... the result.

d I don't get annoyed .... people if I disagree with them. They have their own point of view, so that's fine.

e I'm grateful .... my parents .... letting me make my own choices.

f I'm concerned .... what we are doing to the environment.

3 **In each of the following sentences, <u>two</u> of the options are possible. Which are the two correct options?**

a I watched a programme about people ***who work / who working / working*** in the media.

b This is the app ***showing / which shows / who shows*** how to say exactly where you are in just three words.

c The police want to interview the woman ***who was parking / she was parking / parking*** a red BMW in Lyle Street at 9.17 last night.

d Anyone ***hoping / which hopes / who is hoping*** to do work experience next term must come to the school office at 1 o'clock today.

Summary checklist

I can

- ☐ talk about the kind of work that I and my classmates would like to do.
- ☐ organise and record the results of a survey on the jobs people want to do.
- ☐ say what you need to be good at for certain jobs.
- ☐ understand accounts of inspirational athletes and young achievers.
- ☐ discuss plans and ambitions.
- ☐ write an informal letter.
- ☐ give a talk about the job I would like to do.